All you need to know about DESIGN & DECORATING

W9-CYA-121

Marshall Cavendish

You want your home to look as pleasant as possible — everybody does. And that means decorating, of course — a word that can strike terror into anyone's heart. If this means you then *All you need to know about Design and Decorating* is the publication you've been looking for.

All you need to know about Design and Decorating gives you lots of guidance on design — how to use colour, how to arrange that perfect kitchen, living room, bedroom or bathroom; how to plan for adults and children.

And there are dozens of hints to help you improve your decorating techniques and get the inside professional knowledge on the whole subject.

Stunning photographs in full colour show you the effects you can achieve when you bring the expert touch to design and decorating. And step-by-step illustrations backed up with easy to understand instructions make sure that you are an expert.

Contents

Published by Marshall Cavendish Books Limited
58 Old Compton Street London W1V 5PA

© Marshall Cavendish Limited 1972, 1973, 1974, 1975, 1976, 1977, 1978, 1979, 1980, 1981, 1982, 1983, 1984, 1985

Printed and bound by Grafiche Editoriali Padane S.p.A., Cremona, Italy

ISBN 0 86307 315 8

Design and decorating

Learn to see your home with a designers' eye and you'll quickly find ideas springing to mind that will help you to make the most of its possibilities.

Colour is one of the most important influences on the way your home looks and there are dozens of combinations that will give a room a particular 'feel' or will help you to highlight or camouflage a feature of a room. When you know how to 'balance' and match colours there is no limit to the possibilities — making a 'cold', north-facing room 'warm'; giving a child's room the visual excitement it needs;

solving the specific problems of living rooms and bedrooms, kitchens and bathrooms.

And to your talents for design you'll want to add professional skills at painting and decorating. Imagination *plus* the ability to carry out your schemes will give you a home as beautiful as you desire.

A few vital hints can give you that expert touch that means you can have a go at painting or papering a wall or sticking down ceramic tiles — and getting it right. As you overcome the pitfalls that lie in wait for the amateur home decorator you'll gain in confidence and soon be ready to tackle those trickier jobs — creating patterns in paint; wielding a spray gun; cheering up a dull outside door; papering a stairway; hanging fabrics on your walls; and fixing plastic laminates.

If you've got plans for your home, you owe it to yourself to learn design and decoration.

Colour in the home

Most colours in your life are probably passed by without even a casual glance. They are so familiar to you and everyone else that they are taken for granted. So, when you get down to redecorating, you are faced with a new world: harmonious colours, complementary colours, clashing colours, favourite colours . . . so the question is, 'where to begin?'

But, as with all problems, once you know some facts, then half the battle is over. Facts like whether colours are 'warm' or 'cold'; how they affect each other; which go together without 'fighting'. And also facts about your own house flat or bungalow, since no colour scheme is 'right' or 'wrong' in itself.

What is colour?

The so-called 'white light' we see as daylight is made up of all the colours of the rainbow; it is the mixture of light waves of different wavelengths that creates a white look. The 'wheel' of colour, or spectrum, is made up of red, orange, yellow, green, blue, indigo and violet. The in-between colours with fancy names, so often found on paint manufacturers' colour charts, are made by combining colours, pure and impure. They can be *shades,* colours with black added, or *tints;* colours with white added. You can go on mixing colours indefinitely, but eventually the resulting hues or tints will be too 'close' to be distinguished.

Colour, and the perception of colour, is a complicated matter. For example, what we see as a red cushion is an object which has absorbed all the other colours in the spectrum, and is reflecting just red.

A white wall looks white because it reflects all colours, absorbing none, whereas black absorbs all colours, reflecting none. Black is the total absence of any light or colour.

The brightest, purest colours—red, yellow and blue—are known as 'primary' colours because they are unmixed with any others. Generally, pure colours are strong and vibrant—they seem to shout for attention. Hence, of course, their use for road signs, fire appliances, and other things which must be identified quickly.

The 'non-colour' colours

Black, white and grey, although strictly non-colours, are considered in decorating as colours in their own right. Used together, these three can do a lot for a room, without necessarily having a dull, restrained effect. They also give good functional value when used alone, and in some cases can be quite dramatic.

White, often rightly used to frame doors or windows, separates colours excellently, showing up even pastel tints to good advantage. As well as being fresh looking, it is naturally harmonious. It partners most other colours without a 'fight', and flatters them positively by reflecting its neighbouring colours. A white area surrounded by a dark area will appear to swell in dimension.

Black, although traditionally associated with anything sinister, and with death and mourning in particular, need not be depressing. Small touches of black are usually enough to provide 'drama' for an otherwise weak setting. Ebonized furniture or a couple of black cushions can bring out, by contrast, the richness of other colours. Black-painted woodwork, however, usually ranges from unsuccessful to disastrous in a colour scheme. It can make a room a weird shape, and certainly will not flatter anything in it.

Grey can be used effectively as a background for more brilliant colours, providing a welcome rest for the eye. It can be mixed with other colours to soften them, or used on large areas against which something 'stronger'—an orange sofa, for example—is set.

Black, white and grey have been used together, with splashes of primary colours, by professionals for many successful interiors.

How colour affects you

Yellow is the brightest primary colour, nearest to sunlight and most luminous. Consequently it has a cheering effect, even in winter—but as with all primary colours, if too much is used in a small area it will soon tire the eye.

Red is the most aggressive and demanding colour in the whole spectrum. Used widely for danger signals, it has an immediacy which seems to force itself on you. It is also sexually suggestive, vital (the colour of blood, the essence of life) and advancing. This exhibitionist colour can have an unsettling effect, even challenging, like a 'red rag to a bull'. Mixed with orange and cunningly lit, it can provide an intense warmth for a cold room—a 'Christmassy' feeling.

Orange is also stimulating, but psychological tests have shown that if it is used extensively in a room, the occupants will fast feel 'driven out' by its sheer forcefulness.

Green, the colour of nature, is well known for its restful effect on the eye. In many ways it is the exact opposite of red, in that it is so un-stimulating as to be positively sedative.

Purple, on the other hand, stimulates the brain. Its associations with grandness, royalty and ceremonials can make people shy of using

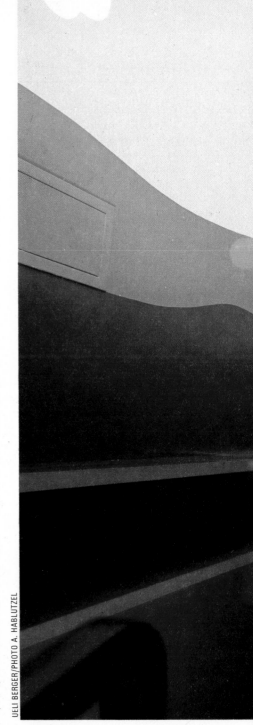

Above. *A landscape in the bathroom—walls and ceiling camouflaged as a background for dreaming while relaxing in the bath.*

it in their homes but, provided it is used in large rooms, it can add a richness and dignity to its surroundings. Used in smaller areas, such as halls, purple can be overpowering.

Brown is restful and, if used in harmony with another 'warm' colour, can make for a cosy setting. Brown on its own, or teamed unimaginatively with pallid cream, can be depressing—as that 1930s craze for 'brown everywhere', a survival from dull Victorian decorating, showed. Brown enjoyed a great revival in the early 1970s, but think carefully before you splash it everywhere; as with

Similarly, oppressively low ceilings can be 'raised' by painting them with soft, receding colours, and high ceilings 'brought down' by giving them a bold, advancing colour.

If you are wallpapering, using stripes is a useful aid to correcting badly-proportioned rooms. Women know that vertical stripes will make them seem taller and slimmer; horizontal stripes will have the opposite effect. The same applies to rooms. Vertical stripes add height to a squat room by carrying the eye upwards, unconsciously beyond the limits of the wall. This may over-correct, though, by making your ceiling seem 'miles away'; in this case, painting the ceiling in a shade of a warmer colour could lower it to the right height. The purer this colour, the lower it will seem. Horizontal stripes add length to a short wall by leading the eye out sideways and 'stretching' the actual distance.

In a room not receiving much light, pure colours can create a sunnier feeling. If you have seen the jewel-like intensity of the golds, scarlets, and indigos which are still to be found in high, dark medieval churches, you will realize that these striking colours would look absurdly garish in a naturally well-lit room. But to darker interiors, they add a touch of richness.

Large picture windows should be framed with a warm colour; in winter, a blue window frame would give the impression of framing the glass with ice.

Angular and aggressive shapes in rooms are more noticeable—and usually considered more of an eyesore—than soft rounded shapes, nooks and crannies. You may decide against ripping out an offending chimney breast, and simply want to 'lose' it by camouflage. In this case, use dark receding colours or gentle patterned wallpaper, while emphasizing the adjoining recess with light pastel shades, or a pure, vibrant colour as a focus for the eye. If you do want to emphasize a chimney breast or some other projection, then reverse the process just described.

As armies have discovered, the best way to be inconspicuous is to dress in the colour of the background they will be patrolling (shades of green in jungles, soft khaki in deserts). If you have a room with many doors which break up the walls into small, ugly areas, camouflage is the best answer for them, too. Paint the doors, frames and all, precisely the same shade as the surrounding walls. If you have papered the walls, then pick out the most retreating, un-noticeable tone from the pattern and paint your doors in it. Radiators or projecting pipes can be camouflaged in a similar way by painting them exactly the same colour as the walls behind.

Equal *tones* will camouflage, even where the *colours* are different. Tones of the same 'weight' will neutralize bad features in a room, whereas a blatant contrast in tone (or intensity) will highlight. Remember that any colour mixed with grey can be used in camouflaging because of its muting, receding effect. Seldom used doors—to store or cellar, say—can be hidden by painting them a deep grey. Alternatively, a shade of your main colour, but deeper and greyer, will help fade them away.

Under-stair cupboards or panelling should, as a general rule, be made to disappear. Darkish colours will help disguise panelling which is

clothing fashions, revivals can go too far.

Blue, as your skin demonstrates in bitterly cold weather, is generally a cold, slightly uncomfortable colour. It has the effect of retreating and, like green, is sedative. Moreover, it is traditionally associated with the chill of holiness. The Virgin Mary's robes, in traditional painting, were almost always blue, and the blue robes of the saints induced feelings of respectful distance, and even melancholia.

Highlighting and camouflaging

Most homes have at least a few good features which can be accentuated by skilful decorating. And almost every home has potential strong points which can be brought out by colour-emphasis.

A cramped-looking room facing the sun can be helped by painting at least one wall in a cool blue or green. This area will seem to 'back away', giving the impression of spaciousness. But beware of using cold colours in a room on the shaded side of the house—you would be just adding to the 'iceberg' effect. It is far better to use pastel tones of a warmer colour. The white in the pastel shades will give the desired illusion of space, while the warm colour will retain its warmth and help correct the room's coldness.

Long, narrow rooms can be given a wider look by painting the shorter walls in warm, advancing colours—tints of yellow, red or orange. Small, boxlike rooms can be made to appear longer by reversing this idea.

Above left. *How one strong colour can create a striking 'wall' from different-sized doors, —and complement the room's other colours.*

Above right. *The neutral cream and white of the low roof beams and walls take the eye straight to the warm-toned seating area.*

HEIDEDE CARSTENSEN/STUDIO HUELSTA

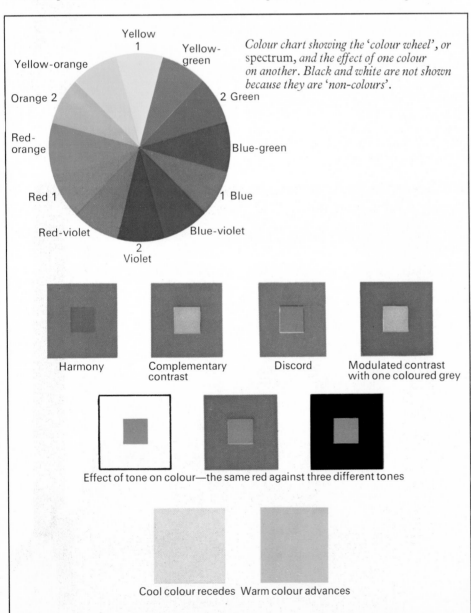

Yellow 1

Yellow-green

Yellow-orange

2 Green

Orange 2

Colour chart showing the 'colour wheel', or spectrum, *and the effect of one colour on another. Black and white are not shown because they are 'non-colours'.*

Red-orange

Blue-green

Red 1

1 Blue

Red-violet

Blue-violet

2 Violet

Harmony

Complementary contrast

Discord

Modulated contrast with one coloured grey

Effect of tone on colour—the same red against three different tones

Cool colour recedes   Warm colour advances

COLOUR PATTERN AND TEXTURE BY WILLIAM GRAHAM/ARTIST LIZ BENNETT

broken up by small doors, or boards which are not well finished. Similarly, the margins beside a stair carpet are best painted in a 'retreating' tone chosen from the colours in the carpet.

Where your skirting board is deep (perhaps 15in.) and in one or two sections or bands, use a neutral colour (grey, light tan, soft beige) on the lower section. This makes the floor space look wider. Then add a crisp, light colour to trim up the upper section, giving a sharp framing line to the wall.

If you have picture rails which you dislike but do not want to remove, you can still make your ceiling interesting by painting the picture rails the same colour as the walls and using a high-lighting colour—the best is always white—on the cornice to frame the walls and ceiling.

Where panel mouldings on ceilings, walls or framing to niches are in good repair, and you want to draw attention to them, apply the highlighting rule. Where they are battered or ugly, apply the camouflaging rule.

So, to summarize the general rule: Use bright, vivid colours to pick out any surface that you like and that projects forward into the room, and use deeper hues on surfaces you want to hide or which are recessed. This magnifies the natural light-and-shade effect of both daylight and artificial light. The projections catch the light, and recesses are naturally in shadow anyway.

The balance of colour

The secret of a professional-looking colour scheme is the skilful use of a *few* colours, or simply many shades of the same colour. The inexperienced person tends to introduce too many colours—giving himself more problems than he can cope with.

To create a harmonious look, there should be a delicate balance among the colours you use. Only a professional designer with precise colour knowledge can deal successfully with discords of the boldest, clashing colours. Large areas of pure colour, such as deep blue walls with a scarlet carpet, can have a very irritating effect. One pure colour should be allowed to be the focus—and if it is a pure colour it *will* stand out, even if used on small areas.

Colours affect each other

Never try to visualize the impact of a single colour on any particular room. Try to see it in your mind's eye alongside the other colours you

MICHAEL BOYS

will be using. Better still, try to get swatches of appropriately coloured card or material; hold them up against walls, furniture and each other. This will help you to gauge how they are going to 'live' together.

If the same colour is used in several places, it will appear to be different in hue, because of variations in the amount of light bouncing off it, and its nearness to other colours. For example, a bright yellow cushion will not look the same yellow on a grey settee as on a tan one. Yellowish-green can make some shades of blue look purple when used close beside them. A very dark mulberry can make a tint of the same colour—such as light mauve—look white. An area painted yellow (the most luminous colour) seems larger than one painted orange (slightly less luminous), and an orange area bigger than one painted red.

A pale grey-green may flatter a room—until you decide to add a *bright* green feature such as curtains, cushions, or an ornament. The grey-green will then 'die', looking very washed-out by contrast.

If you are thinking of an ultra-colourful room, consider how visitors might react. Op-art pictures and decor can have a dizzying effect on people unused to optical illusions. Vibrant colours can be similarly disturbing. But if the *entrance* to a living room is painted in colours complementary to those in the room, it prepares the eye to receive the total colour scheme. This gradual build-up (in some cases perhaps a warning) is known as creating a 'colour climax'.

If you use patterned wallpaper *and* patterned carpet, the room will certainly look smaller. Pattern tends to make even large rooms look 'busy' and cluttered, calling for less furniture in plain designs and colours. As an extreme example, think of the claustrophobic Victorian parlour—a 'jungle' of fussy accessories, surrounded inevitably with heavy, plush-looking wallpaper. Too many bright colours, plus crammed-in furniture, can make a similar impression even in a modern setting.

As with all other aspects of home design, your personal taste will dictate the colours in your home. Rooms that can be categorized as 'trendy' or 'go-ahead' will usually contain some primary colours, stimulating and young in effect. Formal, quiet rooms need a dignified and limited palette. Whatever style you choose, do all you can to ensure in advance that it will please you. After all, you will have to live with it.

PAUL REDMAN

Above. *A whole room decorated overall in muted cream shows how subtle colour can make for an interesting setting.*

Below. *Taking a strong line with a whole wall. The blue and yellow lines framing the wall are echoed in the settee and cushions.*

PAUL REDMAN

Colour for living rooms and bedrooms

Living rooms are primarily family rooms —a homely place to watch television, entertain visitors, and simply relax. As with all other colour scheming, decorating living rooms depends very much on personal taste—and on personality. The danger is in trying to force your particular taste on other members of the family. Many families span a fairly wide age group, with widely differing tastes in colour so that some sort of compromise may be needed if everyone is to feel at home. So try to make colour planning a family decision.

There are other considerations. If you do a good deal of entertaining, and go out a lot in turn, you can afford to be a little bolder in your choice of colours than if you spend most of your time at home and want something more restful. But generally, as living rooms are semi-public in function, you should aim for something more acceptable, to friends and family, than the decor you would choose for a strictly personal room.

If you aim for a restful decor, you might choose soft sage greens, beige, oatmeal—some of the discreet colours. You can buy attractive shades of most colours now. For a more exciting scheme, you might choose whatever are the current fashion colours, and stimulating tints such as white, orange and cerise, or purple, blue and green.

Below. *A warm bedroom setting, using only shades of orange and oatmeal to effect.*

Where to start

Unless you are moving into an unfurnished house, you will probably want to base your colour scheme on some existing feature, if only because it costs less to redecorate a room than to refurnish it. In this case, you should take into account the textures and tones of carpets, a woodblock floor, curtains, light oak furniture—whatever is going to be a permanent feature in the room. This gives you an immediate advantage—as in a crossword puzzle, the first clue solved helps with the next.

Having established the 'base', of unalterable colour, you can build on it in one or two ways. One way, if one colour is predominant, is to build on that colour with a 'tone on tone' scheme. Starting from a blue carpet, for example, you can use other blues—a paler one on walls, a greyer one on woodwork, a greener one for upholstery. Neutral white on the ceiling and on

woodwork trim helps to set off the blues, while accessories in red, orange or black can add dramatic sparkle.

Alternatively, the fixed colour can be part of a complementary scheme. Starting with the same blue, for example, you can make it the contrasting element to soft yellows, corn colour and white, with perhaps both blue and one of the other colours in a patterned curtain fabric.

If a woodblock or planked floor is going to be your starting point, you will already have a large area of rich colour. This can be the trigger for a series of 'natural' colours and materials—hessian for walls in a warm colour; broad striped curtains in browns, greys and off-white; off-white paintwork; Danish rugs in dark brown and off-white.

Which way do you face?

An important consideration is the aspect of the room. Notoriously, a north-facing room has the coldest aspect—although artists prefer north light, because it is the least changeable. South- and west-facing rooms have warm light, and plenty of it.

But all rooms need corrective action to balance out their overall 'temperature.' Adding warm colours—reds, oranges and yellows—helps to overcome the cool north light. Rooms with a south or west aspect, on the other hand, benefit from cool blues, blue-greens and greys, especially where the light is bright and strong.

Colour and artificial light

Artificial lighting does not normally create a colour problem in living rooms and bedrooms, although all artificial light changes the appearance of most colours to some extent. This effect is known as 'metamerism'. Fluorescent lighting can make some colours look 'washed out', while the tungsten filament bulbs most used in homes give a warmer cast to most colours. Normal eyes easily adapt to such slight changes but, when choosing colours, it is a good idea to view them in both daylight and artificial light.

Colour and fashion

Fashion, in colour as in clothing, is a fickle thing. You may decide against 'trendy' colours for that reason.

Keeping up with fashion means almost constant redecoration, since colour fads, wall-covering designs and ideas for using materials change rapidly. The 1960s and early 1970s, for example, saw an upsurge of interest in purples. Then browns, in many shades from beige to peat, became the rage—only to be threatened immediately by an onslaught from sharp lettuce green and deep strong pinks! And while on the one hand there was increased interest in plain textures and natural colours, on the other there was a Victorian revival.

All this shows that fashion for its own sake is only for outgoing people with either great colour tolerance or ample time and money.

Keeping up with progress is quite another matter. Paint and wallcovering manufacturers constantly come up with new colours and textures, and materials of greater durability. It is worthwhile keeping abreast of these developments. Old materials and methods tend to look outdated to the discerning eye.

Colour in small houses

Small houses, flats and bungalows often need the illusion of greater space. This can be achieved by using 'receding' colours such as blue or green, and by creating real continuity of colour. For instance, you could use the same floor covering in all the main rooms. When all the doors are open, a large expanse of floor will seem to open up, flowing from room to room. Muted or neutral colours are best for this, because you can arrange several colour schemes round them—a different one in each room.

Colour for children's bedrooms

Whereas the living room is a semi-public room where visitors are entertained, a bedroom is private territory. This is the room which should be allowed to express the occupant's personality, with no need to 'keep up' with anybody, or to follow any particular fashion at all.

Nurseries, quite rightly, are often painted in pastel shades, or with delicately coloured fairy-tale wallpaper. Very young babies need a restful surrounding, with perhaps just one wall papered with nursery-rhyme or fairy-tale characters, preferably facing them.

As they grow into toddlers, they crave visual stimulation and begin to show a marked interest in the 'loudest' of primary colours. This is when the delicate nursery colours can give way to reds, yellows, oranges, electric blues; children have a built-in tolerance for vibrant colours which adults seem to lack. (On a practical note: remember that toddlers are apt to chew and suck on the corners of furniture, so be careful to use lead-free paints *throughout* their rooms.)

The period between starting school and the early teens often sees a fad for collecting things—almost *any* things. Try not to force more sophisticated patterns on the children's rooms, thinking they will appreciate your tact in implying they are so grown-up. A new coat of paint, or a change of plain colours, will keep rooms smart, but their own accumulations of belongings provide pattern enough.

Teenagers, students and young adults should have a major say in the decoration of their rooms, if not the ultimate responsibility. At this stage, too, their own belongings and bright posters will make a room of thrusting colour and shapes. Usually the bedroom is treated as a private sitting room, with friends visiting—it is, in effect, a bedsitting room. Psychedelic colours and posters are likely to be much in evidence. Whether parents like them is beside the point: colour is a personal thing, and should therefore be tolerated.

Colour for double bedrooms

Double bedrooms are almost inevitably dominated by feminine tastes. Once this meant profusions of flounces and frills, delicate pinks and masses of rosebud pattern. Now there is so much to choose from in both colours and textures that there is little restriction left. A more imaginative palette can make for an acceptably asexual, but still intimate, colour scheme.

Shades of the cool section of the spectrum, such as blues, mauves and aquas, can mingle

Top left. *This inviting room combines the colour of sunshine with the natural materials of rush matting and wicker seats. The dominant colour is picked out in the curtains and echoed by the wallprint.*
Below. *Superbly dramatic bedroom setting achieved with a limited palette. Black and white dominate, unashamedly picking out the strong lines of the furnishings and outlining the shape of the room. Grey is used well to deepen one wall, adding a new dimension.*
Below bottom. *This striking living room employs the blue/green motif to perfection. Usually too sedative, green is enlivened here by splashes of electric blue and bold white furnishings which compel attention. The carpet reflects the green of the leaves.*

"ANNABELLE", ZURICH

effectively to create a cool, sophisticated look, especially if some greenery is provided as a foil.

Pinks still have their place—but these days tend to be allied with salmon, orangey-reds and some pure red to emphasize the warm tones.

All-white bedrooms are always popular, but really succeed only if 'dressed up' with another colour. If the dressing table is the focal point, then its clutter of bottles and jars may provide an adequate splash of colour, as will flowers and perhaps a picture or two.

If you decide on a black and white scheme, then you could paint the walls, ceiling and paintwork white, and use a black rug or bedspread to add drama, and a wall-hanging or two (such as black and white Beardsley prints) to add formal line and dignity. If you have a black wrought-iron balcony, then white alone could give your bedroom a Spanish look. In colder climates, this could be warmed up with bright cushions, vivid ikons, or flowers: in colour scheming, *all* possessions and accessories should be taken into account, since everything contributes to the overall impression. Their shapes liven up the colours too.

Strong greys, deep browns, and restrained colours generally can make a room look 'business-like' and over-masculine. However, if the room is also to be used as a study, this arrangement may provide the necessary compromise between the tidy 'study' look and a restful bedroom scheme. If brown is your central colour, then pretty brown floral fabrics in cushions or curtains could offset any severity. If a deep grey is chosen, then a lighter, brighter colour is an essential to liven it up. A buttercup yellow or bright orange in paintwork trim or fabric accessories, would make all the difference.

Guest rooms

Because guest rooms are primarily 'surprise' rooms, then all types of people with widely differing colour tastes will be staying there if only for short periods. If this always seems a problem when you come to decorate, you could either play safe by using a black-white-grey or brown scheme, or take the bit between your teeth and decorate the room in *your* favourite colours. As a middle course, you can use several shades of one colour, such as green, which will look smart, be restful, and not cause shocked comments or headaches. If you think an all-green room is monotonous, add floral or striped curtains in yellows or orange trimmings. If you start with one colour, you are less likely to make the room look 'fussy', especially as guest rooms tend to be smallish.

HEIDEDE CARSTENSEN/STUDIO HUELSTA

CINDY CASSIDY/PHOTO PAUL RADKAI

Opposite, top left. *A bedroom children would love. The whole room throbs with brilliant primary colours—blue, yellow and bold red. The Mickey Mouse poster echoes the gay mood and the eye is drawn to the floor, where children love to play. Bedtime might even be fun in a room like this!*
Opposite, below. *Bedroom for an older child or for a teenager uses bright, but more subtle, colours than for youngsters. The yellow and orange duvet motif is taken up throughout the room, including accessories such as the giant clock and Beatle posters.*

HEIDEDE CARSTENSEN/STUDIO DIE WOHNFORM

Above right. *A muted, 'mood' effect for a feminine, single bedroom. The warmth of the pinky-mauve is subtly brought out by the period lamp, and the whole atmosphere carefully sustained through accessories.*

Colour for kitchens and bathrooms

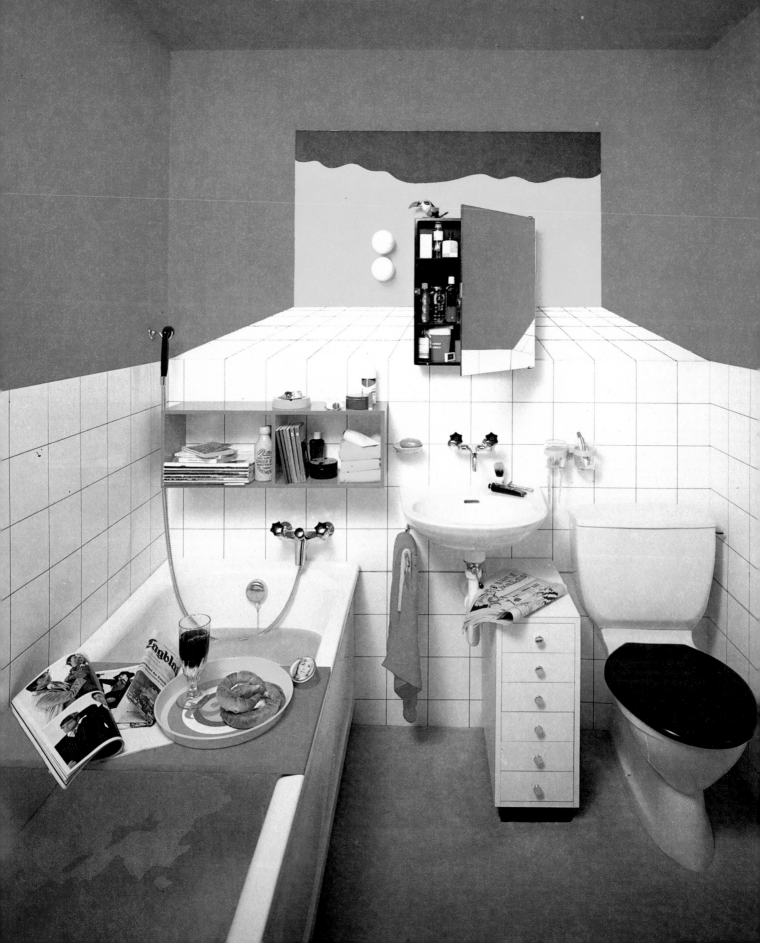

Service rooms—bathrooms and kitchens—have a number of features in common. For one thing their function is similar: they are there for specific purposes, and are not just extra living areas. For another, they take a lot of 'punishment' and have to be hard wearing, which means that they generally need to be redecorated more frequently than other rooms in the house.

Redecorating what are often smallish areas means that you can afford to experiment with more adventurous colours. However, the basic drawback to using wild reds or pinks, or having a black ceiling, is that a family is more likely to tire of such schemes than of the more conventional colours.

Outside influences

Most people have little choice about where their kitchens will be. Modern houses are built with each room to serve a specific purpose, and are fitted accordingly. Old houses in Britain seem often to have been built with the express purpose of putting the kitchen opposite a brick wall. Unless you are altering the back of your house extensively to make the view and access less dark and dingy, then the answer is to paint the kitchen, and such outside brickwork as you are allowed to paint without upsetting the neighbours, in 'sunshine' colours such as yellows and oranges.

'A room with a view', on the other hand, need not be quite so exciting inside. The decoration could emphasize the window, and draw the eye towards it, rather than making the room interior compete with the view.

You could do this by painting the window frame as if it were a picture frame, outlining the view outside. Green or blue paintwork would merge successfully with outdoor foliage, and would also make the window look larger, as these are 'receding' colours. The danger here is in making the room look dull when the view is shut out, but correcting this is easy: you merely use curtains of exceptionally vivid colours or designs. These should be hung on curtain fitments which run well beyond the limits of the window so that in the daytime the curtains can be pulled right back, neither obscuring nor competing with the view into the garden.

Texture for bathrooms and kitchens

Glossy surfaces and gloss paints are often used for kitchen and bathroom walls because people think they are easier to keep clean and are longer lasting. This is no longer true. Today's matt emulsions and vinyl wallpapers can withstand condensation just as well as gloss paint, and are better-looking.

Gloss paints can, in fact, cause a degree of eyestrain by reflecting the maximum light, and tend to condense steam. No surface looks attractive when it is covered with a fine film of mist or, worse, dripping with water. Even a kettle left boiling can cause this very quickly. If

you must use gloss paint in these rooms, try to confine it to one wall only, and not the wall immediately next to the kettle or hot tap. On matt surfaces, on the other hand, condensation is much less noticeable.

The 'balance of temperature'

Kitchens are generally hot rooms, but in older houses can still feel cold and damp, especially if they are on the shaded side. Bathrooms tend to be cool places, in which most people would like to feel warm. These facts should be taken into account when planning your colour schemes for these rooms.

With a cooker, a boiler and sometimes a washing machine working at the same time, the atmosphere in a kitchen—even with all the windows open—can be stifling. So the aim in colour-scheming is generally for coolness. However, it is not necessary to paint the room in wishy-washy colours—dreamy pastel shades will only take away the character of the kitchen and make it look 'institutional'. Bold colours *can* be used, as long as you keep to the cooler section of the spectrum.

A red would give you the impression of cooking in an inferno—you could get away with flame colours only if your kitchen is excessively cold and damp, or is fitted with extremely large windows which can be used most of the year round. So, before you emblazon the kitchen with oranges, reds and yellows, consider the climate and the size and dampness of the room.

Bold brown—with a tiny mixture of orange to alleviate its tendency to be depressing—will smarten up most kitchens, especially when teamed with white trim for the woodwork. Browns with *some* small areas of orange or corn colour can create a cosy, farmhouse-kitchen effect which is very welcoming.

In the bathroom, most people like to feel warm, especially in colder climates. From this point of view, the bathroom could, in theory, be painted bright red all over—all the walls and even the ceiling. This would, of course, create the appearance of a box and even seem to menace the occupant. But a white bathroom with one red or orange wall and matching accessories (such as towels and wall cupboard) will be lively, appealing especially to young children, to whom the bathroom is the least favourite place.

A psychedelic colour scheme, with a large content of potentially disturbing contrast, or lines and colours which are forceful when together, is much better used in the bathroom than in any other room in the house. Each member of the family spends only a couple of hours a day at the most in the bathroom. So instead of the traditional pastel schemes, more 'fun' colours can be used. The peaceful relaxation of hot water can be offset by wild colour clashes and even swirling shapes of green, red, orange, pink or yellow, either in emulsion or psychedelic vinyl wallpaper.

For a dark and dingy kitchen

Kitchens which get little light, or whose shape encourages shadows and dark corners, need colour not only for camouflage but simply to give the room some uplift.

Brilliant white may seem the obvious answer,

but it is an uninspiring one. A simple colour scheme for a kitchen which is facing north, or whose light is shut out by outside structures, could be based on sunshine yellow wallpaper with a white background and a yellow motif. Or yellow flowers with green vinery could be used on one wall—preferably on a large uninterrupted expanse of wall to bring out the full effect of the pattern.

The ceiling and the remaining walls could be painted sunshine yellow, with the exception of the wall behind the cooker or the sink, which could be covered with aluminium tiles. These will catch what light there is and add to it by reflecting the expanse of yellow. It would be a pity to overdo the sunshine effect by adding yellow floor tiles, for example. A dark grey would be a better foil, adding some dignity and depth to the scheme. A yellow carpet or large rug would need cleaning too often, particularly if the kitchen were used as a causeway to and from the garden. A warm patterned orange would be more suitable here. This combination provides a feeling of sunlight, plus a balance of more autumnal colour.

Using pictures

Some of the most successful colour schemes start from a central theme, and are based on the colours in one item. A kitchen is not often thought of as a picture gallery, but, remembering that a kitchen should contain something interesting to look at, a poster is an ideal starting point. Portrait posters are likely to have large areas of facial colours, which might look well on a warm beige-coloured wall with the adjoining walls in navy blue. The floor, by contrast, could be dark green. (This scheme works only in a room which has plenty of natural light—it is out of the question for naturally dark kitchens, which should be highlighted as much as possible.) A rural scene looks well with a dark green wall as a background.

Remember, though, that too many dark colours can be overpowering. If one of the colour schemes above will make your room look gloomy or just too 'strongly' coloured for your taste, try painting one wall a lighter colour, such as a toning blue, green or aqua.

Piping—and other problems

Some kitchens are cluttered, with all their plumbing on show. Water and gas pipes, in particular, always seem to catch the eye unfavourably. You can take a bold line and deliberately 'play them up' as a decoration. It is exciting to paint them all different colours, such as red, white and blue, or red, blue and yellow. A subtler treatment might be to paint them in one tonal or contrast colour, keeping them within the overall scheme.

If the pipe work is rough-looking – or if you are just not brave enough to try the bolder colours – then it would be better to ignore the piping altogether by camouflaging it under some receding colour.

Some permanent kitchen fitments cause colour problems, being far too costly to replace every time you redecorate. Often their colours, especially the colours of plastic work surfaces and built-in units supplied with the house, spoil the main theme. Many standard units are

supplied in pale blues, pale greens or a sickly yellow, and trying to build colours around them limits your whole plan.

If you cannot change their colours, then develop a scheme in which these surfaces become either a sharp contrast, or fade into insignificance by being toned down by other, more vibrant, colours in the same section of the spectrum. For example, a pale blue unit can be made to look pleasant, if not exciting, if the walls are painted dark blue or aqua. On the other hand, if you decorate the kitchen in brilliant white, then the blue unit would assume a more vibrant hue.

A sickly yellow unit could 'work' when made part of an all-yellow kitchen containing many shades and 'weights' of yellows and orangey-yellows.

Work surfaces which come painted in colours which offend you can be painted over, but it is better to cover them with laminate sheeting in a plain colour. This can be white, which is always successful, or a colour which 'picks up' from one of the wall colours and is easily integrated into the whole plan.

The 'pretty' bathroom

For some people, it is fun to experiment endlessly with wild colours and designs for the

Top, left. Cheerful eating area in sunny orange-yellows. Extra spashes of colour are provided by the pinboard cut-outs.
Below. *The last word in space-age rooms. This vast kitchen is entirely decorated in black, and silver, with chrome accessories.*

bathroom. For others, a more feminine or restful approach may be appreciated.

A delicate floral scheme is always attractive, and there are now several ranges of wallpapers with curtains to match. If your family is beyond the stage of having more water on the floor than in the bath, then a luxurious shag pile carpet in off-white or oatmeal will enhance a floral scheme.

Paintwork should pick up its colours from the paper—for example, a matching range which incorporates a white ground with flowers and vines of green repeated in both paper and curtains. This colouring, or just plain white, could be used on the door and ceiling. A bolder approach could pick up the green and deepen it, for trim.

Bathroom accessory colours

The colours of towels and of the bath itself all contribute to the overall decor of a bathroom. Towels are available in brilliant patterns or vibrant plain colours which tone well with the most up-to-date paint and paper ranges. For example, an unusual idea for bathrooms would be to paint the walls alternately red and lilac, using the new paint shades. The door could be painted the same colour as the wall in which it is set, and the final deft touches could be accessories such as towels and wall cupboards in shades of the dominant red and lilac.

Generally, baths look better when they tone in with the overall scheme, rather than being 'outsiders' to it in their usual stark white. Most bath paints are in white only, but baths can be coloured with stains to the desired matching shade.

The sauna look

Although neutral tones do not often make the best scheme for a bathroom, the 'pine and white-washed brick' look has a great following. This is not difficult to create, as wood surfaces need only stripping and covering with a clear polyurethane finish. If you find the stripped wood unattractive, it can be treated with a wood stain. Many people shy away from simulated 'natural' surfaces, but if you like them you can cover the walls with wood grain paper or plastic tiles simulating wood grain, stone or brick.

A 'natural wood look' is best offset with one white wall and a white or pine ceiling. A rush mat makes a good complementary floor covering for this theme, and a venetian blind in natural colours adds the last imaginative touch.

And finally, be bold . . .

In all colour planning, it is essential not to be afraid of experimenting—nine times out of ten, the results will be successful. Even if you do make a mistake, it is rare that it cannot be adjusted by altering the colour of just one wall or the ceiling.

Above, right. The pretty, floral look for an attic bathroom. Dutch tiles and soft off-white adds sophistication to the room where you can feel most relaxed.
Right. Rainbow 'Disneyland' approach for a service room. Imagination and technique can save even bathrooms from being boring.

BRIAN MORRIS

PAUL REDMAN

Learn to paint

It isn't for nothing that carpenters scathingly refer to paint as 'long putty'. Many a botched woodwork job has been rescued by first-class painting. Equally, a bad paint job will ruin the finest woodwork. And come the time that you want a project fit for exhibition —the 'I Did It Myself' show—it is infuriating to see it spoiled by a stray bristle, an ugly run, or worse. Yet careful preparation, and the observance of a few rules, can make your next painting project the most successful yet.

Choosing a brush

A good brush is a good investment—not just in better mileage, but in helping to preserve your good temper. A cheap brush is often stiff, making it difficult to avoid ugly brush marks on the finished job. If the bristles are too thin to pick up a decent load of paint, you may be tempted to dip too deeply into the paint—the result will be a clogged-up brush which you cannot get clean and which will drop flecks of old paint on to the next painting job. And a cheap brush will also shed an infuriating number of bristles—at least a couple of which you will not notice until your otherwise immaculate gloss paint coat has dried out.

To be good, a brush does not have to be the most expensive one in the shop. But its bristles will at least be plump (to pick up a sufficient paint load), soft to the touch (to avoid brush marks), and long (to apply the paint smoothly). The best brushes are those with natural bristle—hair of hog or boar. This bristle has naturally split ends, which provide a grip to hold the paint and help it go on smoothly. Synthetic fibres are smooth and hold paint less efficiently. The bristles on a good brush taper slightly at the end.

General-purpose paint brushes range in width from $\frac{1}{2}$in. up to 4in. For most indoor gloss paint or varnish work a 2in. (50.8mm) brush is easiest to handle, while a 1in. (25.4mm) brush is used for detail work, such as drawer handles and narrow edges.

New brushes shed hairs, and often contain odd bits of bristle and factory dirt. To keep this rubbish out of your painting the brush should be 'flirted', that is, flicked against the hand, and then washed in warm, soapy water and rinsed in clean water. Lay it flat to dry out.

Most professional painters break in a new brush by using it for priming or undercoating. This allows them to deal with the odd stray bristle where it matters least. They also keep one set of brushes reserved permanently for

white or pastel paints, since darker pigments left in the 'stock' (handle) may 'bleed' into lighter paintwork.

Materials required

For painting a whitewood Welsh dresser, the paint tools required are :
1. Paint kettle. **2.** Brushes—2in. (50.8mm) and 1in. (25.4mm). **3.** Glasspaper—grades 0 and 1. **4.** A cellulose-based filler, such as Polyfilla. **5.** Small sponge or duster for surface cleaning. **6.** Patent shellac-based knotting for treating knots. **7.** Thinners—for which to buy, see instructions on the paint tin. **8.** Pva adhesive, which you will mix in a thin solution with the cellulose filler to 'raise the nap'. **9.** A flexible scraper to apply this mixture. Also, you need newspaper or dustsheets to protect the floor.

Wood preparation

Whitewood furniture is made from deal or pine. It sometimes shows knots, it often has the exposed end-grain of plywood showing, especially on door edges, and the timber itself is somewhat coarser than more expensive woods. But careful preparation will give it a uniformly smooth, durable finish.

If the woodwork has any knots, these have to be treated to prevent resin from 'bleeding' through the paintwork. Paint them with a thin coat of the shellac-based knotting, and leave it to dry.

Next raise the nap. Make a paste from 1oz

Fig. 1 (top right). 'Flirting' a new brush by flicking the bristles against the hand. This removes loose hairs, odd bits of factory dirt and any debris from storage before you begin to paint. Starting with a clean brush helps to avoid getting rough patches on the finished paintwork.

Fig. 2 (second from top). Raising the nap by applying a slurry of filler and adhesive as thinly as possible. It is applied to best effect if you work a small area at a time both with and against the grain.

Fig. 3 (third from top). Applying a stiff filler mixture with a flexible scraper to close up deeper cracks, pressing it firmly into the cracks to prevent it from falling out later, and feathering it out over the edges to form a continuous and smooth surface for the paint.

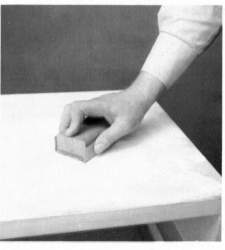

Fig. 4 (bottom right). Smoothing the wood surface by sanding down lightly with glasspaper after the filling dries out.

NELSON HARGREAVES

(28 grams) of the cellulose filler and the same volume of the pva adhesive, mixing with water to the consistency of cream. Apply it to the wood as thinly as possible with a scraper, working both with and across the grain. Work a small area at a time, as the filler hardens rapidly. When this has dried, rub down the surface with grade 0 glasspaper.

This treatment ensures that the surface of the wood is completely smooth. Whitewood tends to swell when moistened and so it is wise to raise any uneven fibres deliberately and sand them down before priming. The filler will also cover any small dents in the wood and close any tiny hair cracks that otherwise would not be obvious until they had been painted over. If any deep cracks are still visible, fill these with a stiff mixture of the cellulose filler and water, following the instructions on the packet. Give it at least an hour to dry—from a pale grey colour, it will turn white—before sanding down very lightly with grade 0 glasspaper.

Before you paint

The traditional three-coat indoor paint method consists of a lead-free primer, with undercoat and topcoat. Buy, if you can, from a store with a fast turnover of paint; pigment settles during storage, so the fresher the paint the easier it is to mix. If in doubt, stand the tin upside down for a day or so before using it, to help loosen settled pigment.

Prise off the lid by levering at several points around the rim, being careful to avoid distorting the tin. If the lid is not airtight, any remaining paint stored in the tin will form a skin. (Any skin in an old tin should be lifted out in one piece by running a stick around the edge; otherwise the skin will break up and leave bits on the paintwork. If necessary, strain the paint through a piece of muslin or old nylon stocking to remove lumps and other debris.)

When you have finished pouring paint from any tin, hammer the lid back on to provide an airtight seal. A block of wood big enough to cover the whole lid makes the best hammer; a carpenter's hammer will sometimes distort the lid and prevent it from closing properly.

Always mix paint thoroughly, with a circle-and-up movement, so that all constituents are evenly distributed. If using a thinners, do so sparingly; too much can spoil both the depth of colour and the gloss. A newly opened tin of paint normally needs no thinners at all.

Left. The simple lines of this whitewood Welsh dresser are enhanced by a smooth and professional paint finish. Using one colour over all, the effect is both homely and sophisticated. The unit can be 'dressed up' to suit your individual tastes and need not be restricted to the kitchen—it is a handsome addition to any living area. When correctly applied, the gloss paint gives the unit a high-quality sheen which is delicate enough to take subtle lighting to good effect. The unit merges well with period or modern decor.

Fig. 5 (top right). Cleaning the unit with a suction head attachment on an ordinary household vacuum cleaner. The surface must be totally free from fluff and dust.

Before you begin work, check the light. Daylight is by far the best, but if you must work at night try to pick the brightest place—the kitchen, probably—in the house. Under poor artificial light it is easy, particularly when using a white gloss finish to leave unnoticed 'thin' patches and spoil the job.

Next, protect the floor with newspaper or dustsheets. Never wear woollen clothes, as loose fibres will settle on the paint. Remove fittings, such as knobs or handles, from the unit. Remove the drawers and stand these on end; it is easier to paint a horizontal than a vertical surface, since there is less risk of 'runs' or 'curtaining'.

Now fix wooden blocks under the base of the unit to lift it clear of the floor. This will prevent your brush from picking up dirt from your newspaper, or fluff from your dustsheets. Vacuum clean the unit to get rid of any dust.

Priming

Always work in a set order. If you live in a house where wood-boring insects are particularly troublesome, start by painting the underside of the unit. It is nearest the floor, and therefore most vulnerable. If not, forget the underside and start on the back—where, while you get into your stride, any faults will show up least—and then do the sides. Next, paint the larger top and front areas and, finally, the narrow dividing strips. Never paint the slides on which drawers run—or they won't.

The primer comes first. Its function is to bind loose particles and form a tough, non-porous surface for the undercoat. Pour into the paint kettle just enough primer to cover HALF the depth of bristle in your brush. There should never be more paint than this in the kettle. By using a paint kettle you avoid the inevitable consequence of painting from the original tin—a build-up of thick, sticky paint around the rim which prevents you from getting an air-tight seal when you close the lid. And, by filling the kettle to the right depth, you avoid overloaded, clogged-up brushes which are hard to clean.

Dip the brush into the primer. Wipe off any surplus paint on the inside of the kettle—not the rim—and lay on the primer with firm strokes along the grain of the wood. Do not be too timid; a firm, wristy action will spread the primer into a thin, but even, coat.

Allow 24 hours for the primer to dry. Then rub it down with grade 0 glasspaper, working

Fig. 6 (second from top). Raising the unit clear of the floor by tacking wooden blocks to the base of the unit. This will prevent your brush from picking up dust from dust sheets, or ink from newspapers, and thus spoiling the painted surface.

Fig. 7 (third from top). Masking tape is used to prevent paint from seeping into the dovetail joints, which could make the drawers hard to open or, possibly, jam.

Fig. 8 (bottom right). Straining off bits of paint flakes and pieces of paint-skin by pouring from the tin into a paint kettle through muslin or an old nylon stocking. Old paint often needs this treatment.

NELSON HARGREAVES

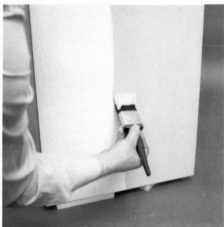

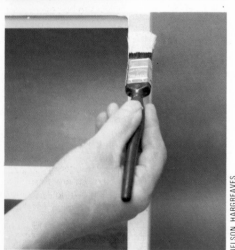

NELSON HARGREAVES

along the grain of the wood, until you have a smooth finish. Wipe off the dust with a rag dampened with thinners. Clean the paint kettle and brush with thinners—the back of the paint tin will tell you which kind.

Undercoating

A good undercoat is, more than anything else, the basis of a good paint job. Any 'pimples', rough patches or unevenness of colour in the undercoat will show through the gloss paint, particularly if this is in one of the lighter shades. So the objective in undercoating is a velvet-smooth surface and an absolute evenness of colour.

White and the reds, particularly, are likely to show up all imperfections. For white, two coats of undercoat are best. For red, the evenness of colour will be improved if a tube of tint colour the same shade as that of the topcoat is mixed in well with the undercoat.

With the paint in your paint kettle at the right depth, dip in the brush and wipe off any surplus on the inside of the kettle. Beginners often make the mistake of dabbing on too much paint too lightly; this causes the ugly, sagging effect known as 'curtaining'. The correct way is to make the paint spread as far as you possibly can while still looking even in colour.

Paint first *with* the grain of the wood, holding the brush quite firmly and without lifting it except where it naturally rises from the surface at the end of a stroke. Without reloading the brush, and pressing much more lightly, work backwards and forwards *across* the grain. This avoids a striped effect by eliminating the first brush marks. Finally, 'lay back'. Holding the brush almost flat with the work, brush so lightly that you can hardly feel the bristles touching the painted area, and in one direction only—with the grain, and working from the newest edge of the paint (the 'wet edge') back towards the previously painted area.

When you load your brush for the second time, start applying the paint, not on top of the existing wet edge, but one brushload away from it, and work back towards the already-painted bit. This avoids a build-up of paint in one place—the prime cause of curtaining. The strokes, on a wide flat surface, should be about a foot or 18in. long.

Fig. 9 (top left). Holding a paint brush in the correct way. Grip firmly and, to prevent unsightly 'curtaining', do not dip the bristles in too deeply.

Fig. 10 (second from top). Applying topcoat with smooth strokes, along the grain of the wood. Breaking the strokes, or dabbing too lightly, will cause curtaining —ugly 'sags' in the surface coat.

Fig. 11 (third from top). Each successive band of paint slightly overlaps the one before. It should be laid on firmly, cross brushed, then finished with the lightest possible strokes. This will ensure that the final finish is smooth and even.

Fig. 12 (bottom left). Tackling the tricky edges with a 1in. (25.4mm) brush.

Edges are tricky; they catch the tip of the brush and release a globule of paint around the corner. Avoid this by stroking *towards* edges, where possible, rather than away from them. If you do cause a run in this way, wipe the paint off your brush and 'spear' off the run by pushing (instead of drawing) the brush. The same trick is used to pick up any stray bristles that appear.

Allow 24 hours for the undercoat to dry. Sand off any pimples, brushmarks or other irregularities with grade 1 glasspaper, and remove the dust with a thinners-dampened rag. If the undercoat is uneven in colour—remember, the gloss coat will probably not correct this— repeat the whole procedure. It is well worth the trouble to get a first-class job. Once the undercoating has been completed, clean brushes and kettle thoroughly once more.

Topcoating

Gloss paint is stiffer than undercoat, so needs to be applied more firmly—although the final laying-off strokes should be, if anything, even more delicate than before. It is important, too, that each new brushload should reach the previous one while the wet edge *is* still wet, and not sticky—with gloss paint, runs and curtaining can happen very easily. Otherwise, the technique is the same as for the undercoat.

One point is worth watching, however; because of its shiny surface, gloss paint can play tricks in poor light, and for this stage of the job only daylight is really good enough.

Gloss paint is touch dry from three to six hours after application, but takes 16 to 24 hours to dry thoroughly. Edges subject to wear or knocks are best left alone for two or three days while the paint really hardens.

Care of brushes

Poor maintenance, tests have proved, wears out paint brushes much faster than painting does—and there is nothing like a dirty brush for ensuring that the next paint job will be a shoddy one.

If you have to leave a particularly long job unfinished in the middle of a coat, brushes full of paint can be left for a day or two suspended in water. Never let a brush stand on its bristles, since this may 'cripple'—distort—the ends. Suspend the brush by slotting a piece of wire or wood dowel through a hole drilled through the handle. For longer periods, of three or four days, thinning agents should be used instead of water. When resuming painting, rough-dry the brush on a piece of clean board to remove excess water or thinning agent. It is important to remove thinners, since they dilute the paint and produce a patchy surface. However, it is always best to finish a coat of paint completely, as resuming the work half-way through will produce an uneven result.

Brushes should be cleaned thoroughly after each change of paint. Working from the stock towards the tip, scrape off excess paint with the back of a knife and sluice the brush in thinners or a proprietary brush cleaner, finishing off with warm water and soap or detergent, and then clean water. Once dry, the bristles should be wrapped in clean newspaper, fixed with a rubber band, and the brush stored flat. Exposed bristles are subject to attack by moths.

Bright ideas with paint

With the aid of a good paintbrush, a non-drip thixotropic emulsion paint and some masking tape, the urge to design with colour and shape can easily be fulfilled, regardless of your technical abilities as a fine draughtsman.

The primary effect of painted walls is usually one of colour, and the secondary effect one of texture. Wallpapers and tiles introduce patterns and more texture. But these decorations may either be too stylized or uniform for your taste, or bear no relation to what you have in mind—decorating a wall in a child's room with a brightly coloured rainbow, perhaps, or painting a freehand mural along a large open wall.

When you decide to paint your own motifs, an infinite number of possibilities can be considered, including circles, squares, vertical and horizontal stripes, triangles, hexagons, and line drawings or freehand drawings of trees, animals, seascapes or city rooftops.

All these shapes, and the colours they are painted in, can influence the entire atmosphere of a room—or they can just be fun to do and to look at.

The advantage of thixotropic paint for painting a wall mural or design is that it is gel-like and quite dense. Usually only one coat is needed over a previously painted surface. Also, once this coat has dried and the masking tape has been removed, the thickness of the paint raises the design to give it slight relief. Thixotropic emulsion paints normally come in both matt and vinyl silk finishes which are simple to apply and easy to clean.

Hard edge painting

One of the easiest techniques to use for decorative painting is known as 'hard edge' painting. It is achieved by painting against strips of masking tape. When the tape is removed a hard edge remains. This process is excellent for abstract patterns, unusual striped effects or even simple line drawings.

The principles are easy and, if proper preparation is taken, the results can be dramatic. Probably the most crucial factor is the condition of the wall surface on to which you are painting. It must be smooth, free from old flaking plaster or paint, and have a solid (not papered) surface. On plasterboard or wallpaper, masking tape is likely to lift the surface. Its surface should first be covered with a high quality emulsion paint such as 'Crown Plus Two' in your choice of background colour, preparing the surface carefully beforehand as any imperfections will ruin the finished design.

One important note: before masking out the

Above. Make a dark corner the highlight of a room with bright colours and swirled shapes.

design on the wall, stick a small piece of masking tape on an inconspicuous place on the wall. Press it on firmly and, after a few seconds peel it away. If the wall surface has been properly prepared, and if high quality paint was used, the tape should come cleanly away without ripping any paint off. 'Sellotape' masking tape, specially made for paint masking, works well for hard edge painting.

Once the surface is ready, you must align the design on the wall. No wall is perfectly straight so it is best to square off the area that you will be covering. Probably the best way to do this is to use a chalked plumb line to mark off vertical lines and a spirit level and pencil to mark horizontal lines. If the design you are planning is at all intricate, it is advisable to trace it out first on $\frac{1}{4}$in. or 6mm graph paper; then mark off the wall area into corresponding 3in. or 76mm squares.

Stripes and patterns

When the wall has been squared off, you are ready to trace the design. Simple stripes can be marked off on to the wall with a pencil, again using a plumb line for vertical ones and a spirit level for horizontal ones. A T-square or try-square may be useful for marking right angles and a set-square for other angles. Involved designs should be transferred from the graph paper to the 3in. squares in their correct proportions.

If possible, use sable brushes of the size appropriate to your stripes or pattern. In most cases a 1in. or $\frac{1}{2}$in. (25mm or 13mm) brush will be adequate. Work quickly and evenly. The ease of working with thixotropic paints is that they can be 'laid' on and do not need extensive spreading.

To create stripes, stick masking tape on either side of the pencil lines you have made and paint the space in between in a contrasting shade.

To create patterns, first stick the tape around the edges of the largest areas to be covered and paint these first. Once the paint has dried, remove the tape, apply new tape to the edges adjacent to the smaller remaining areas, and finish painting these.

As soon as the paint is dry, regardless of the pattern or design you are making, remove the tape by easing the edge from the wall with a handyman's knife or razor blade, and then firmly pulling it back. If you wait too long, the tape will become hard and brittle and will be difficult to remove.

From these basic principles for hard edge painting you can create many different motifs—checks, zig-zags, and concentric patterns. Remember that you paint the area *between* strips of tape and that sometimes, as with checks, you may need to wait for certain areas to dry before you can continue taping and painting adjacent areas.

Spray painting

Painting large surfaces can be a long and tiresome job if you use a brush, or even a roller. If you have a job of this kind to do, it may well be worth while to spray it. Most ordinary types of paint are perfectly suitable for application with a spray gun.

Spray painting is a technique which, if used correctly, can save you a lot of time and trouble in decorating a house. It is suitable for both inside and outside work, and is particularly useful for painting rough exterior renderings such as roughcast and pebbledash, which are hard to paint with a brush.

Spraying equipment can be hired at reasonable rates from tool hire firms. But before you reach for the telephone, consider carefully the kind of job you are going to use it for. For some jobs, it may be far quicker to use a brush or roller.

The first, and most important question is: is it a large, plain surface? For example, if you are planning to spray-paint the walls of a small or medium-sized room with (say) two doors, two windows, a mantelpiece, a fitted cupboard, and the skirting, cornice and ceiling a different colour from the walls, you might as well abandon the project and use a roller. This is because sprayed paint gets everywhere. All the items listed (even the ceiling) will have to be masked with masking tape and newspaper. The time it takes to do this is probably longer than the time it would take to paint the room with a roller.

A large room with few obstructions, however, is quite suitable for spraying. It will save you a lot of time if you paint the ceiling the same colour as the walls. Otherwise, you have to spray the ceiling, then stick paper to the outermost 3ft (1m) of the ceiling adjacent to the walls while you spray them. Obviously, this is time-consuming.

The second most important question is the type of paint you are planning to use. Emulsion paint (interior or exterior) is the most suitable type for spraying. Gloss paint, although it sprays well in the hands of a professional, is

NELSON HARGREAVES

Gloss paint is the hardest type of paint to spray properly. It must be applied in several very light but even coats, or it will run and drip and the result will look terrible.

To spray a door, first mask the surrounding wall carefully, then start by spraying any awkward-shaped mouldings, 1, and the architrave, 2. Work from the top down.

Fill in all narrow strips, 3, then spray the large surfaces, moving the gun from side to side, 4, and lowering it slowly, 5. Then re-mask to spray the wall with emulsion, 6.

very hard to apply without getting drips and runs all over the surface. 'Stone' paints, as used for the outside of houses, can be sprayed only with special equipment including an extra-wide nozzle (to let the stone particles through) and an automatic stirrer (to stop them from settling). This is not normally available on hire.

The third question applies to exterior painting only, and concerns the state of the weather. Obviously, it must be prevailingly dry. No exterior painting, by any method, can be done if it keeps raining. But spraying is also affected by wind. If it is a windy time of year in your part of the world, do not use a spray gun outside the house. You will waste two thirds of the paint, and may easily paint your neighbour's car (and your neighbour, too, when he comes to protest).

Apart from this difficulty, exterior spray painting is easier than interior spray work. There is less to mask, for one thing. Doors and windows must be done, but drainpipes, for example, can be left unmasked and brush-painted afterwards, on top of the sprayed coat, in the colour of your choice. Lawns, flower beds and paving at the bottom of the wall can simply be covered with a tarpaulin or weighted-down sheet of polythene. Hard surfaces such as paving can be masked with a thin layer of earth, which is brushed off afterwards.

Interior preparation

There are no special tricks about preparing interior walls and ceilings for spray painting. Exactly the same techniques are used as for any other kind of painting. Holes and cracks in the wall should be filled, and if necessary, the surface should be primed. Both of these simple jobs are explained in the earlier section on painting. The primer can be sprayed on if necessary, but mask the room (as described below) and read the section on cleaning out the spray gun before you attempt this.

Exterior preparation

Exteriors call for normal preparation, with a few differences. The main one is that nothing on the surface must be loose; i.e. the pointing between bricks must be sound, the surface of rendering must not be powdery or flaky, and so on. If anything is loose, the force of the spray will lift it off and spread it all over the wall in unsightly patterns. This does not show on a rough surface, but on a smooth one the effect is dreadful.

Bad pointing should be hacked out to a minimum depth of ½in. (13mm), or preferably more, and replaced with a mixture of one part of cement, one part lime and six of fine sand, applied with a pointing trowel. Wet the old mortar with a water-soaked brush before you repoint it. Seal new pointing with a sealant

such as Aquaseal when it is dry.

Cracks in stone or cement, or in window-sills, may be filled with a quick-drying cement such as 'ciment fondu' or 'prompt'. The crack should be chiselled out to a 'V' shape to make it easy to fill, and its sides coated with an epoxy bonding agent to make the new cement stick. When repairing a sill, form new edges and flat surfaces by tacking battens to the sound part of the sill with masonry pins to act as a mould. All window sills have a narrow channel called a 'drip' or 'throating' running along the bottom near the front edge. This stops rainwater from running across the bottom of the sill and wetting the wall behind it. Never fill in the drip, and re-form it if necessary by tacking a strip of narrow beading to the underside of the sill to mould a channel in the new cement.

Roughcast and pebbledash that have not been properly applied to a brick wall sometimes fall off in large patches. It is difficult to repair this properly and the repair nearly always shows. But you can generally achieve reasonable results by coating the bare patch with bonding agent and spreading a cement mix on it with a trowel. Use the same mix as for re-pointing. To re-create a pebbledash surface, throw gravel at the wet cement and press it in with your hands.

Roughcast that has been painted before and is flaking should be wire-brushed, then sprayed with a hose to remove the loose particles. Moss

DGW

7

Left. When spraying a flat surface, move the gun from side to side in a straight line, 7, not in an arc. Never stop moving it.
Near right. *Small jobs, such as spraying one radiator, can be done quickly and neatly with aerosol spray cans. The standard of finish will be better than with brushed-on gloss if you spray the paint correctly. Again, do not apply the paint too thickly; three thin coats are better than one thick one. Start with a very light coat along one edge, 8, then gradually work across the area in strips, 9, spraying the remaining edges, 10, before you finish off the central area, 11. Repeat this procedure for as many coats as necessary.*
Far right. *Spray guns have two types of nozzle: the normal round one, 12, and the 'fan' or 'fishtail', 13. The round nozzle's spray pattern has a denser centre, which makes it suitable for spraying narrow strips; the 'fishtail' is better for covering a wide, flat area as evenly as possible.*

or algae should be wire-brushed off too and the affected parts of the wall treated with a strong solution of chlorine bleach to prevent re-growth. Investigate the cause of the outbreak; the wall will probably be damp from a leaking gutter, which should be repaired. You can stop rainwater from soaking into the top of a brick wall by sealing it with a product such as Aquaseal.

Before you spray any type of outside wall, hose it down to remove dust and let it dry thoroughly. A naturally flaky surface, or one that has not been painted before, should be sprayed with stabilizing compound (Blue Circle make a good British type) to hold down loose particles. This also saves paint by making the wall less porous.

You should prepare a timber-clad wall properly before doing any work on it, and also remember to place and fasten ladders correctly if doing any outside work. Check that the ladder is safe before doing any work above head height, and if possible work with a friend.

Masking and protection

Sprayed paint gets everywhere. Anything that you do not wish to be sprayed must be masked thoroughly before you begin—and 'thoroughly' is the operative word. It is no good just hanging a sheet of newspaper in front of an object, because the fine mist of paint will easily float round the back of the paper. It must be properly wrapped in newspaper and the edges of the paper stuck down all the way round with masking tape.

Proper masking takes quite a time and uses a lot of paper and tape. Fortunately, masking tape is not expensive — but do not try to save money by buying cheap tape. Inferior grades stick too well and pull the paint off the surface to which they're stuck. As with hard edge painting, 'low-tack' masking tape, such as 'Sellotape' masking tape, will save you a lot of trouble. Buy two widths: ¾in. (19mm) for holding down newspaper and 2in. (51mm) for covering small objects such as door handles and pipes.

Interior and exterior woodwork, drainpipes and other objects that are going to be gloss-painted later in the course of your redecorating do not need careful masking, and may need

none at all. They will get covered in emulsion paint, but this does not normally matter. Natural stonework, on the other hand, should be masked with great care, because it is very hard to get paint off it. Indoors, particular care should be taken to protect the floor, especially if there is a fitted carpet.

Furniture that cannot be taken out of the room should be stacked in the middle and well covered with dust sheets. A quick way is to use polythene sheets held to the floor with a stapler such as a Rexel 'home tacker'. The staples come out easily when the job is done. Make sure there are no gaps that paint mist can float through.

When painting indoors, take care to give yourself proper ventilation. Mask windows in the open position. You should also protect your lungs by buying a surgical mask and plenty of replaceable pads for it, because the paint clogs pads up quickly. Do not laugh at this precaution; it is really necessary. Paint can give you all kinds of diseases from a mild colic to silicosis.

Any clothes you wear for spray-painting will certainly be ruined. This applies to garments that would not be touched by ordinary painting, such as socks. Remember to take off your wristwatch and any rings or bracelets you may be wearing.

The equipment

Most do-it-yourselfers will be hiring their spraying equipment. The hire firm will advise you about the right type to use for a particular job. Whatever you are using it for, it should operate at a pressure of at least 40lb/sq in. (2.8kg/sq cm). The kind of low-pressure spray gun that attaches to the end of a cylinder vacuum cleaner does not work at all well, so even if you have one anyway, do not use it.

Hire two nozzles for your spray gun: one 'fishtail' nozzle, which gives a wide spray for covering large areas, and one plain nozzle for more restricted spaces.

No doubt the hire firm will give you full instructions about the use of their equipment—after all, it is in their interest as well as yours that it should not be misused. But you may find the following hints useful as well.

Spraying techniques

All types of paint must be diluted with the appropriate thinner to make them suitable for spraying. Emulsion paint should be thinned with water; gloss paint with turps substitute. N.B. turps substitute is very inflammable, so DO NOT SMOKE when spraying with it, and turn off all electric lights when spraying any type of paint.

Thixotropic emulsion paint cannot be diluted and is unsuitable for spraying anyway.

The exact amount of water or thinner to add to any type of paint can only be found by experience. Too little makes the paint too thick, so that the nozzle clogs in a few seconds. Too much makes the paint so thin that it does not cover the surface properly. As a rough guide, emulsion paint should be thinned with half as much water as paint, gloss paint about 50:50 with turps substitute. Experiment on an unimportant part of the wall till you get it right. Even when the paint is the right consistency, the spray nozzle will probably clog occasionally. It should be cleaned out with a very fine wire such as a Primus stove pricker or one strand of an electric flex.

Spray the wall with wide horizontal strokes of the gun, holding it 12-18in. (300-450mm) away from the surface. Move the gun back and forth parallel to the wall, rather than swinging it in an arc. Spray on only a thin coat or the paint will run; you will have to put at least three coats on any surface, but spraying is so quick that you will not waste much time doing this. Gloss paint is particularly likely to run if sprayed too thick.

Every time you stop spraying, even for a few minutes, dismantle the gun and clean it thoroughly with the appropriate solvent (the same as you use for diluting the paint). This is important; once the paint dries, you will have a terrible time getting it off.

Once you have got the spray gun hired and set up, why not use it to paint your garden fence, and perhaps the garden furniture too? On rough outdoor work of this type, a few runs do not really matter much. Wicker furniture can also be given a new lease of life with three or four thin coats of gloss paint. Put everything on a tarpaulin or newspaper before spraying it, though, unless you want a multi-coloured lawn.

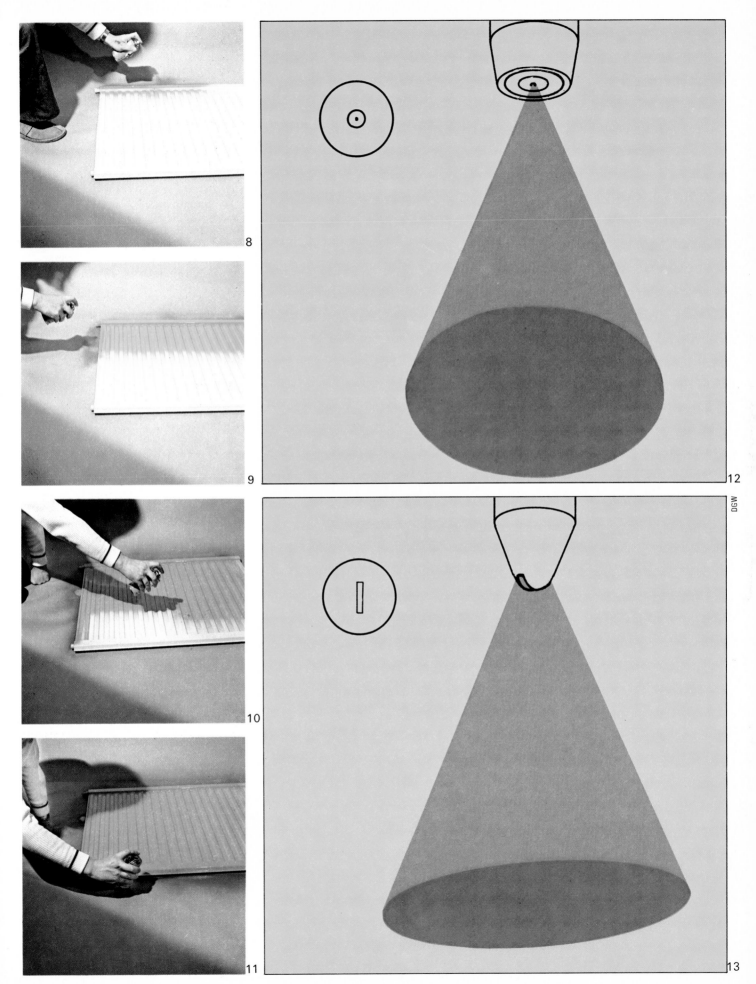

Papering a perfect wall

For your first attempt at paperhanging choose walls which are free of awkward obstructions like doors and windows which might make too many difficulties for a beginner. Move as much furniture as possible from the room, put the rest in the middle and cover it. Give yourself plenty of time—paperhanging can't be rushed—and try to work in daylight.

Materials required

For preparing the walls you will need: **1,** Bucket. **2,** Sponge. **3,** Glasspaper wrapped around a cork block. **4,** Plaster filler. (Use a cellulose-based proprietary brand.) **5,** Lining paper. If your walls were previously papered you will also need: **6,** An old distemper brush. **7,** A broad stripping knife. **8,** Chemical stripper (optional).

For putting up the paper you will need: **1,** Plumb bob, chalked line and chalk. **2,** Scissors with 11-12in. blades. **3,** 3ft or 1m rule. **4,** Soft pencil. **5,** A table or board supported on trestles. (The board should be at least 22in. wide and 6ft long to provide an adequate surface for pasting. An old flush door suspended across two chairs could also be used.) **6,** Adhesive. (Most manufacturers give advice about which adhesive to use for the type of paper.) **7,** Buckets in which to mix adhesives. (Plastic ones are better than metal.) **8,** Pasting brush. **9,** Paperhanger's brush. (Have two brushes, if possible, to save delay if one has to be washed (after picking up paste). **10,** A hop-up or stepladder, plank and strongly built box (to make a platform from which to reach the top of the walls safely). **11,** Seam roller.

Quantities of paper

A roll, or piece, of standard British wallpaper is about 11yd long and 21in. wide. This covers an area of approximately 6sq yd or 57sq ft, but some is usually wasted through cutting and matching patterns. Most papers are ready trimmed but if they are not, this can be done by the retailer. To estimate how many rolls of paper you need, measure the total length right round all the walls you want to paper, and the height of the room from skirting board to ceiling (or to cornice or picture rail). Match these measurements against the chart given below.

Rolls of paper are produced in batches, so check that they come from the same one (each

has a serial number), as rolls from different batches may vary slightly in colouring. If you buy a 'job lot' of paper in a sale, always buy more than you need to cover wastage by matching patterns or through damage.

Preparing the walls

Walls must be carefully and thoroughly prepared in order to make paperhanging a complete success. New wallpaper slapped on top of old is by no means certain to stay up, and is likely to bubble and blister. The walls should be as even as possible, and completely clean and free of grease.

Newly plastered walls containing lime can be papered if they are perfectly dry. Coat the area with an alkali-resisting primer which will neutralize any active lime in the plaster. Alternatively, use one of the papers which have been specially treated for use on new plaster; a lining paper would be useful here.

Distempered walls should be washed down with soapy water to remove all grime.

Painted walls should also be washed down with soapy water to remove all grime. When dry, gloss-painted walls should be keyed by thorough scouring with coarse glasspaper (this slight roughening of the surface will help the paper adhere securely).

Previously papered walls should first be stripped by soaking the paper well with warm water and an old distemper brush. A chemical stripper may be added to the water—but if the chemical splashes the paintwork, wipe it off straight away. While the paper is still wet, use the stripping knife to ease it off a little at a time.

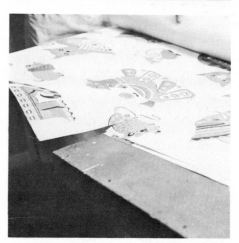

Fig. 1 (top). Folding lining paper concertina fashion makes a long length easy to handle.

Fig. 2 (second from top). Holding the folded lining paper with the left hand leaves the right hand free to smooth it to the wall (reverse this if you are left-handed).

Fig. 3 (third from top). Matching the lefthand side of the paper to the righthand side of the cut piece ensures that a drop repeat matches when the pieces are on the wall.

Fig. 4 (bottom). Using a plumb bob to establish a true vertical line.

ROLL CHART

Height in feet from skirting	Measurement round the walls in feet, including doors, windows, etc,											
	20	24	28	32	36	40	44	48	52	56	60	64
	Number of rolls required											
6 to 6½	2	3	3	4	4	5	5	5	6	6	7	7
6½ to 7	3	3	4	4	4	5	5	6	6	7	7	8
7 to 7½	3	3	4	4	5	5	6	6	7	7	8	8
7½ to 8	3	3	4	4	5	5	6	6	7	8	8	9
8 to 8½	3	3	4	5	5	6	6	7	7	8	8	9
8½ to 9	3	4	4	5	5	6	7	7	8	8	9	9
9 to 9½	3	4	4	5	6	6	7	7	8	9	9	10
9½ to 10	3	4	5	6	6	7	7	8	9	9	10	10
10 to 10½	4	4	5	6	6	7	8	8	9	10	10	11
10½ to 11	4	4	5	6	7	7	8	9	9	10	11	11

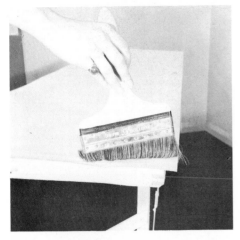

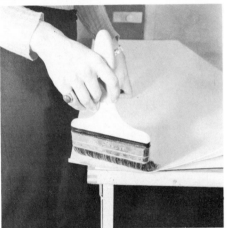

Properly soaked paper will come away from the wall easily and cleanly. Once all the paper is off, wash the walls with soapy water, rinse with clean water and, when dry, sand them lightly to remove surface blemishes, small pieces of paper, old paint drips, and so on.

Making good

Fill any holes and cracks with a proprietary cellulose filler and when it is completely dry smooth it with glasspaper.

The next step is to 'size' the walls. This prevents them from absorbing the paste too quickly, allowing time to position the paper on the walls correctly. To make size, dilute the adhesive you intend to use according to the manufacturers' instructions (the packets usually give instructions for making it up for both size and adhesive). Coat the walls with it, using a pasting brush.

Adhesive

Make up the adhesive according to the directions given on the packet at least 20 minutes before you want it. This gives it time to absorb the water properly and become completely smooth. Always make up a complete packet at a time to ensure a correct consistency—any paste left over can be kept in a completely airtight jar and be used for touching up, if necessary. Don't mix batches of paste.

When the wallpaper is cut, it is a good idea to test for colour-fastness on a waste piece. If the colours do run, take extra care not to get paste on the surface of your cut pieces.

Fig. 5 (top). *Pasting from the centre to the far edge of the paper. The edge overlaps the board to prevent paste getting on to the face side.*

Fig. 6 (second from top). *The paper is pulled back so it overlaps the near edge of the board. The paste is then brushed out to this edge.*

Fig. 7 (third from top). *When the paper on the board is pasted, the righthand edges are brought over to make a large fold.*

Fig. 8 (bottom). *When the whole length is pasted, the lefthand edges are brought over to meet the first fold.*

Lining the walls

For a really first-class wallpapering job, always use a lining paper under the wallpaper. It provides an ideal surface of even porosity, to which the wallpaper and its adhesive will marry, particularly if the wallpaper is heavy (the principle being that paper sticks to paper more firmly than to plaster). Heavy papers, especially embossed ones, have a tendency to stretch as their fibres first absorb the paste but shrink on drying. This can mean that the joints (joins between pieces) open because the paper loses its grip on the plaster surface. Lining paper prevents this happening. Another advantage of lining papers is that they can disguise a 'bad' surface, as well as having some insulating value.

The method of pasting and hanging lining paper is similar to that for wallpaper (see below—make sure you paste the rougher side, so the smooth side is outermost). It is best hung horizontally as the finished effect is smoother. This makes the paper rather difficult to handle on a long wall, so you should fold the paper, without creasing, concertina fashion (always with pasted side to pasted side). Start in the right hand corner of the wall and, holding the paper with your left hand, brush it out with your righthand (reverse this if you are left handed). If you prefer to hang the paper vertically, stagger the joints with those of the wallpaper to avoid the possibility of ridges. Like wallpaper, lining paper should be butt-jointed (ie., the pieces are positioned edge-to-edge, with no overlap).

Using the plumb bob

As few corners, cornices, ceilings or picture rails are really straight either vertically or horizontally, it is wise to use a plumb bob to check them and, if necessary, to establish a true vertical line for the position of the first piece of wallpaper.

The easiest way to do this is to chalk the string to which the plumb bob is attached and then suspend it from the top of the wall, about 20in. from the corner of the wall nearest the light. (As you hang wallpaper, always work progressively away from the light, so that any imperfections or slight overlaps will not cast a shadow.)

When the weighted end of the plumb bob is still, hold it against the wall and pluck the string from the wall and let it snap back to mark

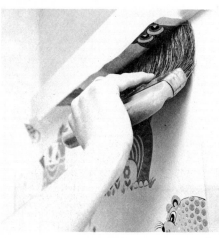

the line (this is much easier to do if someone helps you).

To find a true horizontal line for hanging lining paper, use the 3ft ruler to draw chalk lines at right angles to the vertical. Check the line with a spirit level if you have one.

Cutting the paper

Unroll the wallpaper face ('right' side) upwards. Measure the length required and cut off 2-4 inches below this (the additional amount is for easing the paper at the top and bottom). If the paper is patterned, find the first complete motif and cut off 1-2 inches above. Measure the length, and cut off 1-2 inches below. These extra amounts allow you to position the paper accurately, and to ease it in at the top and bottom.

Cut the next length, checking that the pattern matches exactly at the top and sides, again allowing the additional inches at top and bottom. Lay the cut lengths on top of each other. Cut 2-3 lengths before pasting. Turn the pile over, so that the 'wrong' side now faces upwards, with the first cut length on top.

Pasting the paper

Arrange the pile of paper centrally on the width of the pasting board, so that a little board shows on either side of the paper and the top edge of the paper is on your right. If the paper is longer than the board, have the overhang on your left. Push the top length only so that its far edge slightly overlaps the edge of the board (Fig. 5). This is to avoid getting paste on to the board, and then on to the face of one of the other sheets.

Apply a liberal brushful of paste along the centre of the length of the paper, and brush out to the far edge. Always brush outwards, as there is a danger of paste getting on to the face of the paper if you brush inwards. Slide the paper towards you, so that the unpasted side now slightly overlaps the near side of the board. Brush the paste from the centre to this edge.

When the length on the table has been pasted, lift both the corners on the right edge and bring them over to make a large fold (Fig. 7), without creasing (the pasted sides will be facing). Gently draw the paper along the table until the unpasted portion is flush with the left-hand edge of the board. Paste this length as before and then bring this section over and

down to meet the first fold (Fig. 8).

As each length is pasted, place it on another table to 'rest'. This lets the paste soak in—the time depends on manufacturers' instructions—and the paper becomes supple.

Hanging the paper

Lift the first length of paper over your arm and carry it to the wall. Unfold the top half and, holding the length carefully, place the top edge in position, easing it upwards until the 1-2in. excess overlaps at the top. Keep the side edge exactly level with the plumb line. If the corner is vertical, ease the paper into it exactly. Otherwise let it overlap into the corner.

Smooth along the top of the piece with the paperhanger's brush to hold it in place. Now smooth down the centre and out to the sides in a series of arrowhead motions (Fig. 11). This movement eliminates air bubbles, and spreads the paste evenly on the wall. Don't brush from side to side, as this could move the paper out of position. Try not to overhandle or stretch the paper. If any paste seeps out from the sides of

Fig. 9 (top). *Placing the first length of wallpaper in position, keeping the side edge exactly level with the chalked plumb line while the paper is eased upwards. If the corner is truly vertical, the other edge can be eased into it. Otherwise it should overlap and be trimmed to fit.*

Fig. 10 (second from top). *When the excess paper overlaps for the right amount at the top, the paperhanger's brush is used to hold it in position by smoothing it into the angle of the wall and picture rail.*

Figs. 11 and *12* (third from top and bottom). *Smoothing down the centre of the paper and then out to the sides in a series of of arrowhead movements.*

the paper, wipe it off with a rag. Keep the paperhanger's brush completely clean, and don't let any paste get on to the 'right' side of the paper.

Check again for correct placing, then unfold the bottom section and smooth it out, brushing it as before, until the whole length is completely flat without creases or blisters. The bottom edge will overlap the skirting board.

Run the back edge of the scissors along the paper into the angle between the wall and the cornice or picture rail. Ease the top of the paper from the wall gently, and trim off the excess paper along the crease. Now repeat the procedure at the bottom, where the wall meets the skirting board. If you overlapped the paper into the corner, trim off the excess in a similar way. Smooth the paper back into position.

Hang the next pieces of paper in the same way, butting the edges together (do not overlap them) and carefully matching the pattern. Run the seam roller down the joint to give a completely flat butt edge when the paste is nearly dry.

Above. *A brightly coloured wallpaper, patterned with animal motifs, is ideal for a child's room.*

Fig. 13 *(top). Using the back edge of the scissors to run along the paper in the angle made by the wall and the picture rail.*

Fig. 14 *(second from top). The top of the paper is eased away from the wall and the excess trimmed off along the crease line. The paper is then smoothed back into position.*

Fig. 15 *(third from top). Matching the pattern before smoothing the second length into position. The pieces should be placed edge to edge and not overlapped.*

Fig. 16 *(bottom). Using a seam roller to give a firm butt edge when the paste is nearly dry.*

Papering a
stairwell

The entrance hall of most houses incorporates a stairwell, which makes it a difficult shape to paper. Upper-floor stairwells are also tricky because of their irregular shape, and the difficulty of putting supports on the stairs to enable you to reach the ceiling. But you can overcome these problems if you know how.

The highest walls in most houses are the well walls in the stairwell, and your feet will be some distance off the ground when you paper here. However, as long as you plan your work carefully and do not hurry the job, there is no reason why it should be dangerous. It is of course best to have had some practice in papering a normal room, and you should already be familiar with the techniques involved in simple paperhanging – such as papering a wall – before starting on your stairwell.

Choice of paper

The lengths of paper needed for the well walls in the average house are at least 12ft and often considerably more, much greater than found in the average room. Therefore any difficulties found with a particular type of paper will be more noticeable when papering your stairwell. In particular long lengths of striped wallpaper will show up any corners which are out of true; it is very difficult to false-match such corners. It is easier to disguise out-of-true walls with patterned paper, but you will probably have enough other things to concentrate on when first standing on the scaffold board above your stairs. So if possible choose a random match or small-patterned wallpaper for a stairwell with irregular walls.

Amount of wallpaper

It is easier than it looks to estimate the number of rolls of wallpaper needed if you divide the space into 'boxes' and use the table and method given in the previous section on wallpapering. In your mind, or even on the walls, draw a line extending the landing floor across the stairway. so that you have an upper and lower box. The upper box consists of the entire landing and the section of the stairwell that is above this line: the lower box of the hall and the section of the stairwell below this line.

All the walls in the upper box will be square, so you can calculate the number of rolls of paper needed from the table. Be careful to include the one or two well walls and the head wall in your calculations.

The paper needed for the lower box is calculated separately in the following way. First measure the total length right round the full-length walls in the lower box. Secondly, turn to the walls above the stairs. Just before the staircase begins in the hall, draw a vertical line from the hall floor to the ceiling or to the line drawn from the landing floor. The wall above the staircase is the shape of the triangle formed by the line you have just drawn, the line showing the landing floor and the slope of the staircase. You will need between $\frac{1}{2}$ and $\frac{2}{3}$ of the wallpaper for this triangle that you would need for a rectangle formed by the same horizontal and vertical measurements. Therefore divide the

length of the horizontal side of the triangle by $\frac{2}{3}$ and add this to the total length round the full-length walls in the hall. Then measure the height of the hall and read the number of rolls required from the table. You now have the number of rolls for the complete job, but before ordering your paper carefully consider the following points. In using the table you have used the overall measurements of the walls and not allowed for any doorways or windows. This is because any paper saved by doorways and windows will be used in matching the paper. Therefore if you are using a random-match paper, or if there are a large number of doors and windows you may be able to save on a roll or two. But if you are using a patterned paper which has a 'drop' (pattern repeat) every 3ft instead of the more usual 1ft 6in. (or 1m instead of 0.5m), or if there are unusually few doors, you may need an extra roll or two. If in doubt be on the generous side as it may not be possible later to match the pattern number or get an exact colour match.

Above. Well-papered walls add style to an imposing staircase. Here, the paper tones in with the wooden stair-rail.

It is easy to calculate the rolls of ceiling paper needed from the tables in the previous section, as long as you divide any irregular-shaped ceilings into 'squares'.

Platform safety

Your safety will depend on the platforms you are using, so make sure they are sufficiently strong and properly braced in position. You may decide to buy, or hire from a hire shop, one of the tubular access towers specially made for work on staircases. These can be assembled so that two of the legs are much shorter than the others, and can thus be set up actually on the slope of the staircase. Take care in assembling the units according to the instructions and make sure that the bottoms are securely anchored to the floor. The advantage of these units is that they do not lean against the wall you want to decorate. You may however already have a number of ladders, stepladders and scaffold boards which you use when decorating the other rooms. You can use these instead in the following way.

You will need at least two ladders and one scaffold board for even the simplest stairway, but usually you will need four ladders or step-ladders and three scaffold boards. Check to see that your steps are sound, have no cracks and that the hinges are firmly fixed. Beware if you have painted your ladders—this is an unwise practice as it will hide those tell-tale cracks that warn you your ladders are dangerous. Also check for wear the ropes that keep the two legs of the stepladder from sliding too far apart.

Staircases vary greatly from house to house and the ladders and planks that people already have vary in length and strength. So it is not possible to produce a set of instructions for the platform needed to paper a particular stairway. Instead, the following points are intended as guidelines or hints to assist you in designing a platform for your own needs.

Always try to take your carpets up so that if necessary you can nail strips of wood onto the stairs as stops to prevent ladders from slipping. At the same time check any weaknesses in the stairs – such as a board that has been removed and replaced without being securely nailed in position. This is an ideal time to deal with all staircase repairs.

Single-flight staircase

The simplest type of staircase consists of a single straight flight of steps between two solid well walls with a small landing at the top. Above the stairs and between the well walls is the head wall. The platform for this type of staircase is shown in Fig.1.

Place a short stepladder or packing-case on the landing so that a board can rest on one of the steps and extend horizontally over the stairwell to within a foot or so of the head wall. To support the other end of the board take a short ladder or a tall stepladder with the legs tied firmly together. Place the foot of the ladder on the staircase and the top against the head wall so that it leans away from the slope of the staircase as in Fig.1. The ladder must never be at an angle flatter than 45 degrees to the vertical, otherwise its strength will be impaired and it may break.

Double-flight staircase

A staircase consisting of two flights of steps which turn through a 180 degree bend and double back is illustrated in Fig.2. It is similar to that found in many houses.

The triangular and square steps at the bend do not provide enough room for a stepladder, so the system used for the single flight (Fig.1) cannot be used for the lower flight here. Instead, lean a ladder against the wall at the top of the first flight of stairs with the foot on one of the stairs (see Fig.2)—check that the ladder is not flatter than 45 degrees. Nail firmly or screw a strip of wood, say, 2in. x 2in. (50 x 50mm) to the tread of the stairs and rest the foot of the ladder against it to prevent it from slipping.

In place of a head wall there will be a banister. If it is a good strong one, you can rest the other end of the plank on it. If, however, it is lightly constructed, it may not be strong enough to take the weight. In this case use a short stepladder or large box on the landing instead. The system so far described is most suitable for preparing the

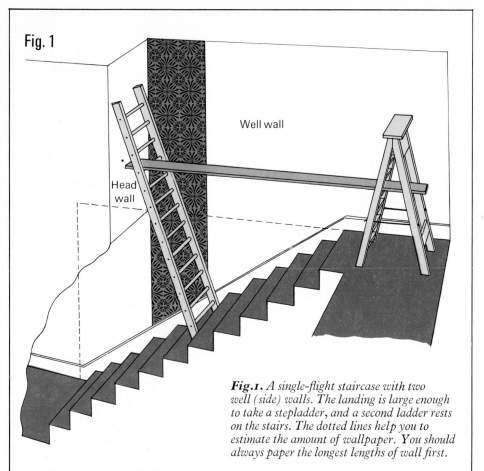

Fig.1. *A single-flight staircase with two well (side) walls. The landing is large enough to take a stepladder, and a second ladder rests on the stairs. The dotted lines help you to estimate the amount of wallpaper. You should always paper the longest lengths of wall first.*

Labels in Fig. 1: Well wall, Head wall

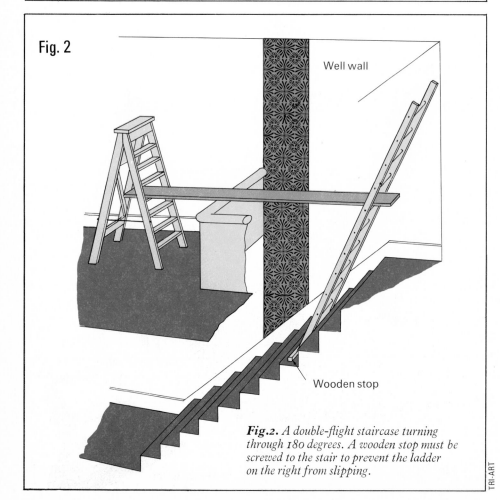

Fig.2. *A double-flight staircase turning through 180 degrees. A wooden stop must be screwed to the stair to prevent the ladder on the right from slipping.*

Labels in Fig. 2: Well wall, Wooden stop

Above. *Colourful wallpaper and contrasting paintwork add warmth to an entrance hall. The white stairs and door add light to the scene.*

well walls, as there is no ladder leaning against them and getting in the way of your papering. The same system would however not be suitable for papering the wall at the top of the first flight of stairs.

To paper this wall, a ladder is leant against each of the well walls and a board placed between them leaving the wall to be papered free of obstacles. In the situation shown in Fig.4, a stop must be nailed to the appropriate tread of the stairs to keep the right-hand ladder that rests on it from slipping. The other ladder rests against the riser of the step and is thus prevented from slipping away. The step at this bend may however be rather narrow, especially for the wide foot of a stepladder. In this case just turn the ladder upside down (tie its legs together first) and rest the narrower top of the stepladder on the stair.

When papering your stairwell you will use both these systems at different times, depending on which wall you are papering. When stripping and preparing the walls, however, a combination of both systems is normally used, as shown in Fig.5, so that you can reach all the walls without moving the ladders.

Order of papering

Normally the walls and ceiling in any room are papered beginning near the window and working away from the light. This is to prevent any shadows being cast by overlapping joints. With a stairwell, the same order of papering applies only as long as it does not conflict with the following requirements.

It is usually advisable to paper the ceiling so that the strips lie in the same direction as the scaffold boards you are using. If, as in Fig.5, two of the boards run with the stairs, the ceiling paper must run in the same direction; if the paper was hung at right-angles to the scaffold boards it would be easy for you to slip between them.

The walls should always be papered starting with the longest length of wallpaper even if this occurs directly opposite the window. You can then begin by hanging the longest length vertically, using a plumb-line. If you began with

Above. A double-flight staircase opens on to a small landing. The open-type banister gives the impression of greater space.

a shorter piece any deviation from the vertical would be accentuated when you hung the longest piece. There is also the advantage that you can take the longest lengths from new rolls and can use the end of the rolls for the shorter lengths. From the longest length of paper work in both directions until both pieces meet in some inconspicuous part of the hall and landing, such as above a door.

Papering around banisters

All the basic papering techniques have been described in an earlier section. With the longest pieces of paper you may need to slide the paper up or down to match the pattern at eye level — otherwise although it matches at the top it may be fractionally out at eye level, owing to the paper stretching.

With a stairway, there is often the added complication of a handrail on the wall. If possible, always remove the handrail from the wall before papering. As you paper over the screwholes, press the paper firmly against them and make a hole in the wallpaper with a nail so you can locate them later when you replace the banister.

With a double flight staircase you will have a banister in place of a head wall, as in Fig.2. The longest stretch of wallpaper is usually next to this; if so, align your first strip of wallpaper against the banister. You may have to cut a small piece out of the paper where the handrail widens at the top. The next strip of paper along the upper landing will have to be cut to go around the banister. Paste the whole strip and starting at the top of the wall, hang the paper until you reach the top of the banister. In the edge of the paper that touches the banister, make a scissor cut about 1½in. below the top of the banister and sloping upwards diagonally as in Fig.4, followed by two more small cuts across the first cut as shown. This will allow the paper to be laid lightly in place around the banister. Run the back of the scissors down the angle between the banister and the wall. Then quickly before the paste dries, lift the paper from the wall, cut along the scissor mark, and brush the paper back in place.

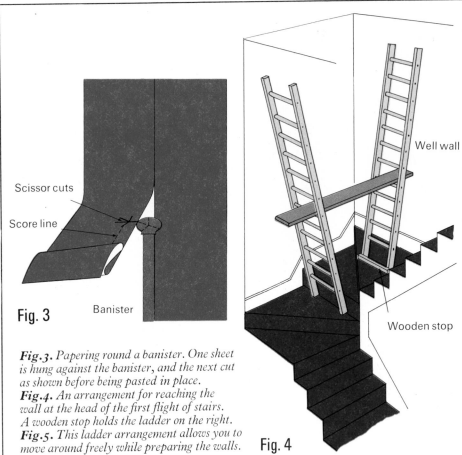

Scissor cuts

Score line

Fig. 3

Banister

Well wall

Wooden stop

Fig. 4

Fig.3. Papering round a banister. One sheet is hung against the banister, and the next cut as shown before being pasted in place.
Fig.4. An arrangement for reaching the wall at the head of the first flight of stairs. A wooden stop holds the ladder on the right.
Fig.5. This ladder arrangement allows you to move around freely while preparing the walls.

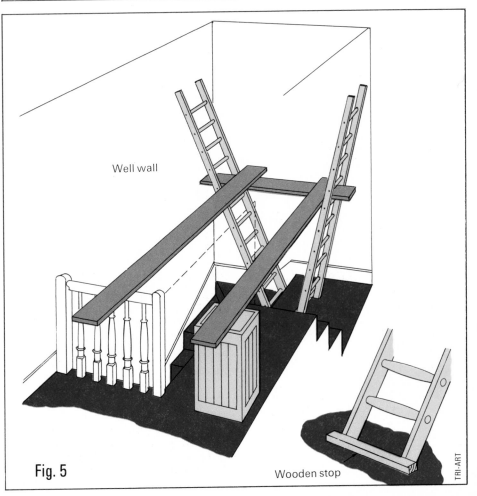

Well wall

Fig. 5

Wooden stop

Staircases and landings

The staircase is the backbone of a house, and it should hold its whole colour scheme together. The hall gives the colour key to the downstairs rooms, and the first-floor landing to the upstairs rooms, so the staircase is the link which co-ordinates the decorations used throughout the house.

If you are standing in the hall and looking through open doors into all the downstairs rooms, the colours you can see should blend with what is used in the hall. The same applies to the landing or half landing; you can use the colour scheme on the stairs to make a subtle colour transition from ground floor to first floor.

In this way your home will gain a closely-related visual unity. It will have a central colour scheme, rather than being a series of separate rooms behind doors that have to be kept shut to avoid an ugly clash.

Co-ordination

It is often more economical to use the same carpet throughout the hall, ground floor rooms, stairs and landings, so you could do worse than to make the stair carpet the basis of the colour scheme of the whole house. Beware of using too strong a colour if the carpet is to go in one or two rooms as well as the circulation areas, because it may make your choice of related colours for use elsewhere somewhat complicated.

A good choice of colour for a stair carpet, for example, is beige. Blend it with a warm chestnut brown wallpaper in the hall, up the stairs and along the landing. Use crisp white paint for the doors, all woodwork and the ceiling to maintain a feeling of spaciousness.

An enormously wide range of colours can now be mixed to your requirements by most leading paint firms, so you have plenty of scope when you want to choose colours that will tone with the basic one for the different rooms leading off the landing. For example, one child's bedroom would look gay in orange, another in apricot and white; you could have brown cork tiles and more white in the bathroom, and yellow and white for another bedroom.

Another good basis for a colour scheme is a multicoloured wallpaper up the staircase, or a patterned carpet. You can then pick out various different plain colours from the pattern for each of the rooms leading off the hall or landing.

Left. If you can't hide your staircase, make a feature of it by picking out the outline of the steps and painting the banisters in a contrasting colour.

Colour scheming

There are many ways of adding character to unprepossessing small staircases and landings, and one of the easiest and most effective ways of doing this is by a suitable choice of colour.

You can transform a narrow, dark staircase and pokey landing in one of two ways to great effect. The first, and more obvious solution, is to make everything seem more spacious by choosing bright, clean colours like white or soft pastel shades. Keep any patterns simple and small—choose a delicately patterned wallpaper on a white background rather than one in outlandish geometric figures. The woodwork should also be white, with the minimum of fussy detail.

In places like this, curtains waste space, and look as if they do too. A plain blind at the landing window can be either the same colour as the paint, or in a fabric to match the wallpaper. If you do want to add pattern to avoid a stark appearance, you can use a border paper, either just above the skirting board, or along the top of the walls. This treatment can also be applied to the blind using wide patterned fabric tape to link it with the scheme. The carpet should also be in a pale colour.

The second method is to aim at a more dramatic effect and not try to deceive people into thinking there is more room than there actually is. For this, choose dark colours and rich patterning; look for art nouveau wallpapers in deep rich colours, dark blues, purples and browns. Paint the ceiling in the darkest colour of the paper and choose the same colour for the carpet. Put a blind or curtain made of matching fabric if possible, or a plain toning colour, on the landing or staircase window. You can make bright pools of light with spotlights trained against the walls, and the whole house will take on a complete different atmosphere.

Making a feature of the stairs

You can make the ground floor of your house look more spacious by knocking down the partitions separating the living room from the hall and staircase (provided they are not load-bearing; you then need planning permission). The staircase is now incorporated into the living area, and is ready to be made into a focal point or main feature of the decorative scheme.

If you are turning the ground floor of your house into an open-plan room in this way, you can give more space to what might be a narrow, unattractive staircase, or even put in a new one. One of the modern 'open-riser' type will look well here. There are many good ways of making the staircase look less bitty and linking it with the room.

On an open-riser staircase, for example, fix the carpet not only on to, but right around each tread. If you fit glass shelves into the angle of a staircase, you can use them to display ornaments and make a feature of the half landing.

If you have very high ceilings, a large and noticeable handrail running up the staircase wall can break up the large expanse of wall and help improve the proportions. A different colour above and below the rail, or perhaps a patterned wallpaper above and a plain colour below, will increase this effect.

You can sometimes pick up lovely old stair furniture such as handrails and banisters in houses that are going to be demolished, and these can be used to transform a plain staircase very cheaply.

Stair carpets

On a narrow staircase it is best to have a full-width fitted carpet; not only is it safer, but it also makes the stairs seem wider than they are. In most houses, the stairs are 31in.-32in. wide, but standard stair carpet is normally 27in. wide. In order to make your stair carpet fitted, therefore, you have to use the next width up (36in.) or fill in the extra space. This can be done by joining a small additional section on one side of the main width, or by fitting a small addition of equal size on each side of the runner. The added strip can be in short sections for economy, with the joints hidden in the inside angle of the steps.

Stair carpet must be fixed very firmly to ensure that it does not work loose. It will inevitably get fairly rough treatment, but the wear will be spread more equally if you move it every six months.

Handrails and banisters

Many of the accidents that happen in the home occur on or around the stairs, so it is essential that handrails and banisters are completely stable. Safety is all the more important if there are children or old people in the house. So don't make any modifications that might make the banisters shaky or hard to hold.

If you strip the old paint off handrails and banisters in an old house, you often find surprisingly attractive wood underneath. You can make a solid rail from planks of wood nailed to the staircase wall, so that there is some support on both sides.

Spiral staircases

A spiral staircase takes up rather a lot of space, but if you have the room it can look very attractive. Look out for decorative old spiral staircases made from wrought iron. They are in fashion at the moment, which makes them expensive in most places, but you may be lucky if you keep your eyes open. You can make a focal point of an iron spiral staircase by painting it in a brilliant colour, which will really make its decoration stand out.

If you have a large attic room, a spiral staircase can be a most attractive way of reaching it, but if you have very little space, a ship's ladder of tubular steel with firm steel handrails can be as effective. If a retractable ladder is what you need, buy one of the many light modern loft ladders, which unfold at the touch of a finger and can easily be stored away in a small space.

Children and staircases

Make sure that any paint or wallpaper that can be touched by a child as he goes upstairs has a practical washable surface. The staircase wall is particularly vulnerable, and is one that can be seen by visitors (unlike nurseries, which can be shut off from view when necessary). If the paper is not washable, coat it with a special clear protective coating such as Fend.

Safety gates are essential for busy mothers, allowing them to work without worrying unduly about a small child wandering all over the house. If you spend most of the day downstairs, fit the gate at the foot of the stairs. It must be impossible for a child to open the gate, but the lock must not be too fiddly to undo in an emergency like a fire. Special locks are made for this purpose.

Landings

Landings and half landings are often ignored when it comes to decorating a house, but if treated with imagination, they can be not just attractive, but useful features.

You can make a narrow landing look wider by papering or painting the wall along one side of it in a colour that contrasts with the other side. Don't put a mirror at the far end of a narrow landing, it only makes it seem longer; instead, put it on one side, or even on doors opposite each other, thus giving a feeling of increased width.

On a square landing with doors leading off the sides, put a large mirror covering the entire wall opposite you as you walk up the stairs to it to make it appear twice as large.

You can make a tiny landing look more spacious by painting or papering the door panels to match the surrounding walls.

A large landing in a small house may have enough room to hold a collapsible spare bed, which can be disguised as a chair or sofa when not in use. A window seat in the form of a low, shallow chest or stool set below a window with its curtains arranged to hang open all the time will give a feeling of increased depth to a half landing, but don't put too much furniture there; spindly occasional tables will only clutter it up and get in the way.

Some landings are big enough to use for light storage; you could have a small desk and drawers for filing. If the landing is not draughty, it can quite easily become a sewing, mending or ironing corner. It should not, however, be devoted to homework or any task involving concentration, as people going up and down the stairs will cause disturbance.

Smaller landings can become display corners; one large toy such as a rocking horse or doll's house, which would otherwise take up valuable storage space in a toy cupboard, would look attractive at the head of the stairs. You can turn a half landing into a library corner by fitting shelves along one or two walls, or display a collection of special ornaments or china on them.

Space under the stairs

If you have an open area under a flight of stairs, there are endless uses to which you can put it. In an open-plan room it can become a pleasant sitting corner with a fitted sofa. Paint

Above. If a staircase is part of a room, its colour scheme can be incorporated into the other decorations. Here a striking modern design has been used to camouflage the stairs.

the wall and sloping ceiling under the stairs in a dark colour to give it a cosy, alcove-like appearance.

If you have a young baby, all its large equipment can be stored here; pram, push chair and any large toys. It can even be a daytime sleeping corner for a baby; it can be screened off with a small folding screen covered in fabric to match the walls or curtains.

This area, too, is ideal for a sewing or working corner, as a desk or sewing table can often be fitted neatly under the low part of the sloping ceiling, with a light fixed on the wall above. If it is suitably placed, it can become a tiny playroom where the children can be supervised by their mother while she is working in the kitchen; a blackboard could be fixed to one wall. There will still be plenty of room to store toys and drawing or painting things under the lowest part of the slope.

If the space has already been closed off or made into a cupboard, it can provide vital storage for tools, paints or house cleaning things. If there is enough height, you can fix up a rail for hanging coats with racks for boots and shoes in the low part. People who make their own wine will find a closed-off stair cupboard specially useful, as it supplies a large, dark area that is reasonably warm—just right for fermentation.

Lighting

Carefully chosen lighting can transform a dull, narrow staircase or landing into a spacious, attractive area. A central hanging light is the easy answer to the problem of lighting a staircase, although it is not the most original treatment.

Whatever lighting you choose must for safety reasons be bright enough to give a clear view of every stair, whether you are going up or down. Wall-mounted lights can be effective, but they should be fixed above shoulder height, so that no one will knock into them. Spotlights arranged to highlight each landing give a spacious effect to a small staircase.

Remember that anyone walking upstairs towards a hanging light with a conventional shade will look straight into a bare bulb. Avoid this by using a globular shade, or one that hides the bulb with a fringe. If there is enough space

on a landing, you can make a pleasant view up the stairs by putting a small table at the top with an attractive table lamp on it. But don't place it so that people knock into it.

Borrowed light

You can gain more light in a dark landing and staircase by fitting glass panels in the doors leading off it. A large mirror at the corner of the stairs or on a half landing can be used to reflect the light on to a dark area of the landing; it will also give an impression of more space.

If you cut a small 'archway' window in the staircase wall giving on to a light room, this will lighten the staircase considerably. You can use frosted glass for privacy if this is needed.

Ideally, the staircase should be lit by a window in an outside wall. Even a small window over a staircase or landing will give it a fresh, spacious appearance. Don't clutter up the window with nets or frilly curtains or pelmets, as they will reduce the amount of light that enters. Blinds are the best answer, as they let in the maximum amount of light and don't get dirty as quickly as curtains.

Pictures

Pictures can be used to lessen the closed-in

Above left. This landing and staircase has been made lighter and more spacious by the use of white paint over large areas and a delicately patterned wallpaper in places.
Above right. A shallow half landing can be given importance by hanging full-length curtains permanently open, and displaying a plant in an attractive pot in the window.

feeling that many staircases have. On a narrow staircase with walls on each side, hang pictures only on the walls where the staircase turns, and at the top and bottom, rather than up each side. If you cram the side walls with pictures, it will only make the staircase seem even narrower, and the pictures could easily get knocked by people walking past them.

A tiny portrait or sketch displayed by itself will not look interesting, but a collection of attractive small pictures grouped together will give people something to look at as they walk up or down the stairs.

On a larger staircase you can have a freer hand, but there are still pitfalls to guard against here. If you have an artistic bent you could paint a large mural over an entire landing wall, or 'cheat' by using a huge photographic reproduction of a landscape to give an illusion

of increased depth to a landing.

Posters can be used to brighten up a large bare wall very cheaply, and pictures arranged in vertical rows can counteract the feeling created by a long narrow landing.

Flowers

The final touch to any room or decorative scheme to give it a lived-in feeling comes from flowers. Fresh flowers improve the look of any corner, and there is always enough room for a vase on a small stool or table at the head of the stairs.

You can display a collection of pot plants on a light, draught-free landing; this is a very good way of cheering it up in winter when cut flowers are expensive.

A half landing is a perfect display point for an attractive jardinière, which might be a completely wasted minor feature elsewhere. Window boxes on inside or outside sills will cheer up an uninteresting view out of a landing window as well as adding a splash of colour to the stairwell. A tub containing trailing plants will fill awkward corners in a landing. Make sure the tendrils don't trip you up, though; after all, stairs are primarily for walking up and down, and your decorative scheme should not make this impossible.

Above. *A multi-patterned arrangement of ceramic tiles makes both an unusual and a practical wall finish for a bathroom.*

Wall coverings to suit all tastes

Walls account for the largest surface area of a room, making the choice of a decorative finish very significant.

Whether it be mosaic tiles, flock wallpaper or vinyl paint, the finish will influence the entire room's character.

The choice of wall decoration is dependent upon suitability of appearance, amount of maintenance needed, and cost. Living areas and bedrooms, for example, have relatively minor maintenance problems and the choice for these rooms is likely to be made mainly on the basis of the colour, pattern and texture required for the particular room. A painted or wallpapered surface might be the most likely choice, although other appropriate finishes could be wood panelling or boarding.

Rooms which are liable to high humidity,

such as kitchens and bathrooms, need a more durable surface capable of withstanding water splashes, detergents or grease marks and regular cleaning. Tiles, plastic laminates or, in the less vulnerable areas, vinyl wall coverings, would be suitable choices for these areas.

Paint or wallpaper?

In rooms that do not require a particularly durable surface, and have suitable wall surfaces (such as smooth plaster with no cracks), the least expensive wall decoration will usually be a painted finish. This may also be the best choice on other grounds. The advantages of paint are that it is readily obtainable from stock without special ordering, inexpensive, can be applied by a competent handyman, and it is the least frustrating way to obtain the colour you want. With wallpaper, hours of searching through pattern books may fail to produce the colour required in a suitable pattern. But with paint the availability of a wide range of standard colours and the facility for precise mixing of special colours make it possible to obtain an exact choice.

Mistakes can be corrected more easily with paint as well. If you find, for example, after hanging one or two pieces of wallpaper that the scale of the pattern or the general effect is not as anticipated, it will be necessary either to live with your mistake, or to reject the whole supply outright and buy fresh stock. If, however, a sample panel of paint indicates the colour is strong or the hue needs adjusting, it is a simple matter to mix in the appropriate corrective colour.

Always prepare a test panel and check this before proceeding with an entire room, since a small pattern on a colour card can give a false impression of the effect over large areas.

Varieties of paint

All paints are basically similar in composition —consisting of a pigment mixed in a suitable medium, with various additives to improve certain qualities.

Hard gloss oil paint uses linseed oil as its medium, mixed with pigment, a thinner to improve workability, and a drier to speed up drying. A traditional finish for woodwork, it is usually applied to walls only when a durable, washable surface is required. Before beginning to paint it is essential that the wall is dry, since the paint forms an impervious film which will not allow moisture to evaporate; if dampness is present, it will normally cause blistering and flaking of the paint layer.

Because it is non-absorbent, a gloss paint surface on walls or ceiling in a room subject to high humidity will cause condensation—in severe cases water will collect and drip from the ceiling and run down the walls. It is not, therefore, a very suitable material for kitchens and bathrooms, although in the past it was often used in these areas because of its washability. Today, however, there is a wider choice of more suitable finishes, made from various synthetic resins and marketed under different trade names. Condensation in kitchens and especially in bathrooms will occur to some extent, no matter what type of wall covering you choose to use.

Enamels formerly meant paints designed solely for applying to metal or clay surfaces which are fired at high temperatures to produce a stoved finish (vitreous enamel), but the term is often used loosely today to describe a superior hard gloss paint for normal use. It is especially good to use on flush surfaces such as cupboards or on areas where a fine finish is wanted. Most gloss paints can be thinned with mineral turpentine substitutes, but it is important to follow the manufacturers' directions as some have complex compositions.

Emulsion paint is, in some cases, an adequate alternative to gloss paint. Apart from its tendency to induce condensation, a gloss paint finish is often unsuitable for walls because of its shiny appearance, which emphasizes any slight irregularities in a wall surface. Most interior walls look better with a matt or slightly glossy eggshell finish.

The development of emulsion paints, in which particles of the medium are dispersed in water, represented a great advance for the home decorator, since they combine the advantages of a flat finish oil paint with the convenience of a water paint for thinning and cleaning of brushes. Most modern emulsion paints are composed of a synthetic resin emulsified in water. The finished surface of these paints is very durable and will withstand frequent cleaning.

Even more resistant to dirt and moisture are co-polymer or plastic emulsion paints such as those which provide a vinyl finish. These form a continuous surface of plastic 'skin' and must be applied to walls that are smooth and free from grease, flaking paint and paper. *Oil bound water paint*, or distemper, is similar to conventional emulsion paints, but is cheaper and not nearly as durable.

Acrylics represent the latest development in emulsion paints and can be used almost any-where—even on damp external walls.

Thixotropic paints are 'jelly' paints with a dense medium which thickens the consistency of the paint, largely eliminating the problem of paint drips. A further advantage to the handyman is that the increased thickness of the paint film results in a greater opacity, so that one coat is often sufficient to produce a uniform tint. The most professional looking results, however, will be obtained by building up several thin layers of paint. Thixotropic paints come in a wide range of colours in gloss, emulsion and vinyl finishes.

Cellulose paints must be applied with a spray gun for best results and are not very suitable for domestic use. They are best used on metal and other surfaces which will need a high gloss finish.

Stone paints have small particles of stone mixed in an emulsified resin base. Their normal use is for external brick or rendered surfaces, but they can be used internally to improve the appearance of a brick or a cement rendered wall.

Many other paints have been developed for special situations. These provide rust, damp, fungus, fire, or acid and alkali resisting finishes.

Varnishes and sealers are used where exposed natural surfaces, such as wood, stone or slate, need protection. They are transparent and usually based on linseed oil or polyurethane resins. When the natural surface is to be retained, but the colour needs improving, a varnish incorporating a stain can be used.

Primers. To obtain a smooth finish, the top coat of paint must adhere thoroughly to the wall surface. Some surfaces, such as old plaster, may vary in their porosity, and if a top coat paint is applied directly onto this surface, it will produce a patchy finish. Primers, therefore, are used as base coats to provide uniformly absorbent surfaces for later coats of paint, and to seal in alkalis or other chemicals which might affect the decorative finish. Primers are usually white or pink.

Undercoats. One or more coats of undercoat are usually necessary on new walls to build up the colour to a dense uniform level. Normally they are fairly thin, but have a high pigment content to give good opacity, and they dry to a matt finish. Existing paint, if it is in good condition, will need only one undercoat and one top coat in most cases. It is important, however, to ensure that existing coats are adhering properly and are being uniformly absorbed. Be certain that new paint is compatible with the old paint you are working over, as some paints react with chemicals in other paints.

Wallpapers

If a texture or a pattern is preferred to a flat colour, some form of sheet wall covering is indicated. The cheapest material of this type is wallpaper. There are several different kinds of paper available in an incredible range of patterns.

The largest selection is still to be found in the standard range of wallpaper with flat printed patterns. These include stripes, abstract forms, geometric shapes, floral and pictorial patterns and regular small-scale designs which give the appearance of texture. Patterns are often available in a choice of colourways.

An increasing number of wallpapers are now treated to make them spongeable. Some are even claimed to be washable, but the extent to which a printed paper surface can be cleaned is inevitably limited; if severe dirtying is likely, a more durable surface should be selected.

The range of patterns available in ready-pasted wallpapers is also steadily increasing. These are generally more costly than standard wallpaper, but may offer savings in time, effort and equipment.

Wallpapers with an embossed texture to simulate a woven fabric, or with other raised patterns, are useful for covering walls or ceilings with uneven surfaces or with minor plaster cracks.

Some extra-stout embossed papers have patterns which stand out in high relief. These can be used very effectively with oblique lighting, which will emphasize the pattern by casting strong shadows. They are best used in small areas to accentuate a panel of wall, rather than as a general surface over an entire room.

There are several other variants on the basic print paper finish. Some manufacturers produce a range of papers with a metallic surface. These often have patterns of stripes or geometric shapes embossed on the surface, which produce varying degrees of reflection from different angles. They should be used with caution as they can be overpowering and too showy. For many rooms the wall surfaces, while looking attractive in themselves, should act as a background for the furnishings. Too strong a colour or pattern on the walls can

produce a harsh and disjointed effect. Often, therefore, metallic papers are used to their best advantage when restricted to small areas, like corridors, where a more dramatic effect is required.

Flock papers are made by printing the pattern in a glue and dusting the surface with fine shreds of coloured felt which adhere to the surface, and produce a raised velvet effect. They are a modern imitation of handmade papers of the eighteenth and nineteenth centuries and, as such, they are used in rooms which seek to reproduce this period. The designs tend to be traditional and rather large in scale and are not really suited in modern, bright and clean interiors. They are also expensive and need careful hanging to ensure that the pattern in adjacent lengths matches.

Vinyl Wallcoverings

In kitchens, laundry rooms and bathrooms where water may splash on walls, or where it will need frequent cleaning as in playrooms, a surface which can withstand regular wiping down is needed. The new vinyl-faded wall-coverings are excellent here. The vinyl surface is available on either a paper or a fabric backing of these, the paper-backed types are cheaper and quicker to hang, as they need only a heavy-duty paste. The fabric-backed types normally require a special adhesive, but they are more stable and less likely to stretch unevenly in the hanging process. Some vinyl wall coverings are available ready-pasted.

The extensive choice available includes plain colours and patterns with a flat surface, or embossed surfaces that simulate canvas and other fabric finishes. Some patterned vinyl with coverings tend to be rather large in scale, and these can be used successfully only on a large wall.

Other materials

Many of the following suggestions for wall coverings are dealt with in greater detail in a later section — this section dealing solely with the selection of materials available and how to use them to their best possible effect within the home.

One of the high quality, and consequently more expensive wall finishes is *hessian.* Being naturally woven fabric, a hessian covered wall has a warmth and character quite distinct from that of vinyl and paper decorations, but has the disadvantage of being difficult to clean.

Another rather costly, but high quality, wall finish which offers an unsual and pleasing appearance, is composed of very thin slices of *decorative hardwood* mounted on a flexible backing. The thinness and small size of the wood pieces enable the paper to be hung in the same way as woven materials, again using a special adhesive. It can also be used loose as a screen or blind.

Natural grass papers enjoyed popularity some

Decorating an uneven wall surface can present problems
Top left. *A brick-walled vanity area painted with several coats of white emulsion.*
Bottom left. *A feature brick wall covered with a special copper foil.*

years ago when they were first introduced from the Far East. They are composed of strips of natural decorative dried grasses stitched to or mounted on a backing and are hung in the same way as the woven fabric described above. Being a natural product, the pieces vary slightly in width, thickness and colouring, but it is precisely these qualities which give grass papers their distinctive character.

The surface of grass paper is surprisingly hardwearing, but it is not easily cleaned due to its coarse texture, and it is expensive. If, after some time, you wanted to change the decoration and paint your walls, you would have to strip off this paper, as it cannot be over-painted. The same also applies to woven fabrics and the hardwood material.

Tiles

The best surface for areas which must stand up to regular cleaning with detergents is *ceramic tiles*. These are made of fired pressed clay which is then glazed and fired again to give a high-gloss or matt finish. They come in an enormous range of plain or mottled colours.

There is also a choice of tiles decorated with screen-printed patterns. Some of these are self-contained designs and can be mixed into a wall of plain tiling to add a decorative effect. Others are designed to form a continuous pattern, while still others, based on Spanish or Portuguese handpainted tile designs, can be used either individually or as part of a regular repeat pattern.

Above. *Papers and paints are always available, but it is often fun to try something new. This simply designed bedroom has a single*

These tiles are usually about $\frac{1}{4}$in. or 6mm thick and $4\frac{3}{4}$in. or 110mm, or 6in. or 152mm square, with various other sizes available to order. Tiles with one or more rounded edges to fit around wall perimeters are also manufactured.

Relief tiles, which have a pattern moulded into the surface and are usually glazed with a plain colour, are also available in sizes similar to those above, but these are about $\frac{1}{2}$in. or 13mm thick. As with heavily embossed papers, they will be seen to best advantage if lit from one side or from above to produce a strong 'modelled' effect.

Tiles are traditionally fixed by bedding in a cement and sand mortar mix on a hard, flush surface, but one of the proprietary mastic adhesives may be quicker and easier to use. The joints are pointed in plaster or portland cement, unless there is any danger of movement in the surface to which they are fixed. If this is the case, a mastic compound should be used.

Polyvinyl chloride tiles are made in sizes similar to ceramic tiles, and are also available in panels moulded to simulate a group of individual tiles. They are fixed with an impact adhesive and are good to use in bathrooms, since their warm surface reduces the likelihood of condensation. The surface is, however, more liable to damage by scratching and knocking than a clay tile, and will not withstand abrasive

wall covered with cork tiles, such as are used on floors. The result is a subtly textured wall that blends well with the colours of the room.

cleaners, such as detergents or scouring powders.

Another attractive and suitable wall finish for bathrooms is *mosaic*. The true vitreous mosaic composed of a small square of glass or vitrified clay is very expensive, but *ceramic mosaic* with an eggshell finish and various other cheaper types are available. These are usually sold in panels about 1ft or 300mm square, covered with a temporary paper facing which is washed off after the mosaic is fixed.

Like ceramic tiles, they can only be fitted to a hard flush surface, and are fitted with adhesive in the same way. The joints between the pieces are filled with white cement or other recommended grouting medium after the paper has been removed. Generally, the pattern of small pieces provides sufficient visual interest, and panels of uniformly coloured pieces are preferable to those with a mixture of colours. Some manufacturers produce panels composed of cushion-shaped square pieces, rectangles or hexagons.

Bathrooms usually need at least one *mirror* and the opportunity can be taken to form part or the whole of a wall surface as a mirror. Apart from its practical use, a large wall mirror can be effective in increasing the apparent size of a small bathroom, especially if it extends the full width of the wall at eye level.

A conventional, silvered plate glass mirror can

UELI BERGER/PHOTO A. HABLUTZEL

Above. Bathrooms, usually being quite small and fitted with awkwardly shaped fixtures, are a challenge to decorate. This confining *bathroom is painted all over in a warm red paint and decorated along one wall with mirrored cabinets to give an illusion of space.*

be used, but this should not be fitted above a bath or other source of steam, or it will quickly mist over with condensation. This can be overcome by using a sheet of silvered plastic which is marketed at approximately the same price as the glass type. Glass mirror can also be obtained in the form of tiles which will fit in with the pattern of ceramic tiling.

Stainless steel, an increasingly popular surface for sink-tops, utensils, dishes and tableware, is also available in tiles and can often help to relate the walls to the other surfaces in a kitchen.

The other popular material for vulnerable areas of kitchen walls is *plastic laminate sheet.* Laminates come in a wide choice of plain, or mottled and marbled colours, woven and geometric patterns, and woodgrains. They are made from compressed layers of resin-bonded paper, topped with a layer carrying the printed decoration and a clear melamine coating.

It is a very versatile and durable material and can be cut to most shapes. Impact adhesive can be used to fix it to any rigid smooth backing, such as blockboard or chipboard. The edges of the backing material are usually lipped with matching laminate, which is available in strips about 1 in. or 25mm wide in a variety of popular colours. The surface is very hard and tough and will withstand regular cleaning and normal

domestic liquids. A cigarette resistant grade is also obtainable.

Since laminates can be used for tabletops and worktops as well as for wall facings, it is possible to feature a consistent colour and pattern scheme which will help to give the room a unified appearance.

The very thin, *flexible vinyl sheeting* which usually comes with a self-adhesive back protected by a cover piece, is not suitable for permanent wall facings or splashbacks: its use should be restricted to covering shelves and other areas where splashing and high humidity do not occur.

A similar material which is available mounted on hardboard, however, could be used as a wall facing. It is fixed by nailing to wood grounds plugged to the wall, or by glueing with an impact adhesive to a hard, flush surface. The wearing characteristics of this surface would not, however, approach those of plastic laminate sheet or ceramic tiles.

In some rooms, such as a child's playroom or a study-bedroom, pinboard wall panels can serve a useful as well as decorative purpose. Inexpensive insulating fibreboard sheets, nailed to wood grounds or fixed with plaster dabs to the wall, can be used and can be painted or faced with a vinyl wallcovering.

A more durable and more expensive wall of

this kind can be made from a suitable floor finish, such as cork tiles, or linoleum. Cork tiles can be fixed with adhesive to a smooth surface. Linoleum, (which should be heavy quality, at least $\frac{1}{8}$ in. or 3mm thick) is obtainable in tile form which can be similarly fixed, or in wide sheet form which should be stuck and pinned to a rigid backing of blockboard or chipboard. The composite panel is then fixed to the wall by screwing into wood grounds or plugs. The panel should be trimmed with a narrow hardwood moulding.

Design considerations

Every room is a separate problem, and every family will have its own views on the most suitable treatment. Generally it is wise to spend plenty of time deciding on the colour and material. When choosing a material for a wall decoration, any shortcomings of the room should be borne in mind.

Avoid cheap material or tools; they often take up more time than better ones and can lead to poor results.

Do not skimp on preparations. Tiling on an uneven wall will never look satisfactory, and a painted surface will ruthlessly reveal inadequate preparation and undercoating.

Take into account the use and wear the surface will receive and select the material accordingly. It is very disappointing when a whole room is spoiled by one or two vulnerable areas which will not stand up to everyday wear, and tear.

New ways with fabrics

Fabric has long been a popular form of wallcovering, but it can also make an attractive alternative to painting or varnishing parts of furniture, such as drawer fronts, doors, bath panels, blanket boxes, bedheads, shelves, waste baskets, lamp bases, and screens.

Covering surfaces with fabric is different from actually *making* a cover for the item because the fabric is attached by adhesive or tacks, and there is no sewing involved.

Fabrics used this way are hard-wearing and practical; they can be cleaned by brushing or vacuuming and, with the exception of felt, they can be 'refreshed' by gentle sponging with a damp cloth. Almost any fabric may be used, but some are more successful than others.

Hessian. This is made from jute and is available simply as furnishing fabric in widths up to 50in. or paper backed specially for wallcovering in a 21in. standard wallpaper roll or in pieces by the yard between 30in. and 39in. wide. It is probably the most popular of all fabric wall-coverings, and looks particularly good in alcoves and as a background for paintings. Of the two kinds, the paper backed is more expensive but has the advantage of being easier to hang because it gives the hessian body and prevents it from distorting or wrinkling much. It is not available in as many colours as furnishing hessian, but there are a variety of weaves. Some are treated with a special process which keeps the weave straight and helps to prevent fading—a snag of furnishing hessian. Both kinds can be emulsion- or gloss-painted satisfactorily.

Linen. This is made from flax and, like hessian, is available by the yard as a furnishing (or dress) fabric in a variety of widths, or paper backed and 30in. wide. It is softer than hessian and, although the unbacked kind should be hung in the same way as hessian (see below), the backed version is hung like a standard wallpaper because it is thinner.

Felt. This is available in rolls for wallcovering up to 72in. wide and in a tremendous range of colours. It is fairly easy to use, although heavy, and is particularly good as a sound insulator. (It is also good for cupboard and drawer fronts because it is firm and does not easily fray or stain from adhesive—provided the adhesive is applied carefully.) It should not be used in a sunny position, because it fades.

Silk. The most commonly used types are moiré and slub silk. Silk should always be paper backed for use with adhesive because otherwise the surface would be spoiled by the adhesive seeping through and staining. The paper backing also gives it some body when being used as a wallcovering. It is very expensive, however, about five or six times as much as a good wallpaper. Even though the 30in. wide rolls are sold with instructions, it is difficult to use because it is untrimmed—and trimming is not easy because of the natural variation in weave—and because the slightest mistake (rough handling or uneven application of adhesive which seeps on to the face of the fabric) can ruin a whole wall length. For this reason, manufacturers usually stress that it should be hung by an expert (there are many professional decorators who baulk at it), and they will often recommend specific people. It is worth following their recommendations because if anything goes wrong the silk will be replaced free of charge to you.

Grasscloth. The beautiful rough texture is achieved by sewing together dried grasses of various thicknesses which are then stuck on to a paper backing. Like silk, it is very expensive and although it is possible for a non-professional to hang the lighter kinds quite successfully, many of the same problems apply and it is worth having an expert to do it.

Cork. Not strictly a fabric, it comes into the same category because of its delicate, textured effect and because it is applied in the same way. It is made in rolls 30in. wide, specially for a wallcovering, from wafer-thin cork shavings which are pressed on to adhesive-covered paper.

Carpet. To use this as a wallcovering would have seemed ludicrous at one time—and also

too expensive and heavy. However, it is possible and practical with self-adhesive carpet tiles and is actually recommended as a wallcovering by the manufacturer. It would probably be too oppressive on more than one wall in a room, but it does give warmth and virtual soundproofing.

PVC fabrics. With so many vinyl-coated wall-papers available, it is not worth using pvc fabric as a general wallcovering. However, for other small areas it is very practical because it is strong and easy to clean. It is very easy to use in the self-adhesive versions, as the adhesive is 'activated' either by removing the paper backing, or by soaking in water, depending on the make.

Treated fabric. If you want to use ordinary dress or furnishing fabric to cover large areas of wall, it is worth having it specially treated by the Alphacol process. Almost any fabric—both natural and synthetic fibres—can have the treatment, which is a form of plasticizing that stiffens the fabric but without making it shiny or affecting its appearance in any other way. Any shrinkage occurs during the stiffening process, and not when the fabric is applied to the wall; the fabric can be sponged clean and will not fray. It should be used with the adhesive supplied by the manufacturer who treats the fabric. This adhesive should be applied to the wall as for other fabric wallcoverings (see below); because it is slow drying it gives more time to position the pieces but without any danger of seepage. Any bubbles can be ironed out—with a hot iron—when the adhesive dries.

Methods of attaching fabrics

Wherever it is possible (in panels for a door front or blanket box, for example), it is better to attach the fabric to the surface by tacking it down because, unless the fabric has been treated, shrinkage is one of the main hazards of using adhesive. If adhesive has to be used—for a wallcovering for example—each piece of fabric (including paper backed ones) should be cut 1in. wider and 2in. longer than the area to be covered (this extra should be allowed for when calculating the total amount). Shrinkage can be reduced if the adhesive is put on the surface being covered, rather than on to the fabric back or paper backing. To ensure that any shrinkage is even, the adhesive should be rolled on smoothly. Applying the adhesive to the surface also helps prevent the staining of the fabric through seepage.

Manufacturers of paper backed fabric wall-coverings usually recommend which adhesive should be used for their particular product. It may be a heavy-duty standard wallpaper paste, such as Polycell Plus, or a thick prepared paste, such as Clam 143. For unbacked and untreated fabrics, Clam 143 or a not-too-sloppy adhesive such as a thick pva or an adhesive with a latex base may be used. It is always wise to test it with a small piece of fabric first to make sure that it

Below. Textured fabric wallcoverings make an ideal setting for paintings and give extra interest without being obtrusive.

will bond the fabric and surface together satisfactorily, that the adhesive does not seep through, and that the fabric's colours do not run. A lot will depend on the type and weight of the fabric, how much dressing (starch) it contains, and the temperature of the room. In a cold room, the fabric will take longer to dry out and there is more chance of shrinkage.

Whatever the surface being covered—even if the fabric is preshrunk—all joints should be butt-edged following the method given below. (With treated fabrics, the edges should be butt jointed as for wallpapering.) If you are covering something with a tricky shape, make a paper pattern first and try it for size before cutting out the fabric.

Fabric as a wallcovering

You will need all the tools used for normal paperhanging — plus a heavy 6in. rubber roller and a foam-sleeved paint roller for applying the adhesive.

Prepare the walls and, if using an unbacked fabric, line the walls with a toning paper to prevent any patches showing through, particularly at the joints. To prevent fraying, use a sharp pair of scissors—or a sharp knife and a straight edge—to cut the pieces (allow the extra for shrinkage). Do not stretch the fabric or pull at any loose threads—these can be cut off later.

Next, mark with chalk a plumb vertical line on the wall for the first length at a distance from the corner of 1in. less than the fabric width.

Continue marking vertical lines along the wall at the same interval of 1in. less than the fabric width. Using the foam roller, apply the adhesive to the section of the wall for the first length of fabric only, to within 1in. of the line.

Position the first length so that one edge is level with the chalk line and there is a free 1in. overlap on the other side at the corner and at the top and bottom of the piece. Pat down the length with your hands and then smooth it down with the rubber roller, working from the centre towards the sides. Do not roll too heavily, or the fibres may become distorted, and do not trim off the excess fabric yet. If using felt, roll the length on to a batten and suspend it between two step ladders. Allow overlaps as for hessian, press it on to the wall at the bottom and work upwards.

Making a butt edge

Roll the adhesive on to the next section of wall and then hang another length of fabric, overlapping at top and bottom and on the side of the first length that you hung. Hang all the remaining lengths in the same way, leaving the overlaps loose and untrimmed.

When the adhesive is dry, flatten the loose edge on the join and, with a straight edge and sharp knife, cut through the centre of both pieces (be careful not to gouge the wall). Remove the waste strips. If you are using felt, tease the edges slightly to fuzz the join. Paste the wall immediately under the join and press the fabric down into position. Then trim the top and bottom edges, and the corner overlap, to fit. Use a seam roller with great care, as it can cause stains if pressed too hard.

Applying fabric to panels

Where fabric is being used simply for panels, it can be stuck on as for a wallcovering or it can be tacked inro position. The tacks can be covered with cut-out frames of $\frac{1}{8}$in. thick plywood, or with a beading, or with a braid edging.

Plywood frame

Use a fine-toothed panel saw to cut the plywood to the overall size wanted; sand the edges smooth. Mark the area to be cut out, and remove it with a sharp handyman's knife. Fill in any holes with cellulose filler; when it is dry, sand the edges smooth and paint the frame.

Cut the fabric to the same size as the inner edge of the panel, plus $\frac{1}{2}$in. all round for the frame to grip it firmly. Tack the fabric to the surface you are decorating with flat-headed tacks or staples. Apply a strong all-purpose adhesive to the back of the plywood round the edges and/or the surface to be covered (see manufacturer's instructions) and then cover the fabric with the frame. Use adhesive tape to hold it in position until the adhesive dries.

Beading edging

Any design of wood beading or moulding may be used, providing it has a flat base and it is wide enough to secure and hide the edges of the fabric. If the panel is on a door, the frame should be 1-2in. from the edges so the door can close. Mark out, on the surface you are decorating, the area of the frame (ie, the line to which the *inner* edge of the beading will be placed) and cut two lengths of beading the length of the frame height, plus 2in. If you have a mitre block, use it to cut off both ends of one piece of beading so that they slope inwards at an angle of 45°

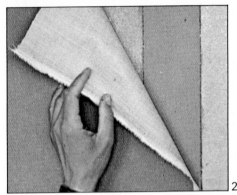
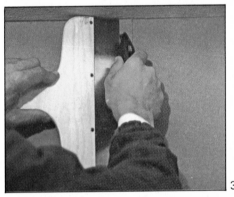

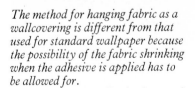

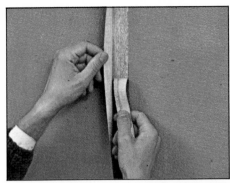
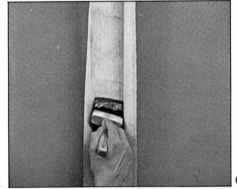

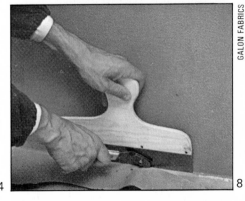

GALON FABRICS

The method for hanging fabric as a wallcovering is different from that used for standard wallpaper because the possibility of the fabric shrinking when the adhesive is applied has to be allowed for.

Fig.1 (*top*). The adhesive is spread evenly on the wall for one 'drop' at a time, to within 1in. of the plumb line.

Fig.2 (*second from top*). The adhesive for the next lengths should be applied carefully, leaving uncovered the sections where the pieces overlap.

Figs.3 and **4** (*third from top and bottom*). When the lengths are hung and the adhesive is dry, a cut is made through the middle of the overlap, using a sharp knife (or special weave cutter) and a straight edge.

Fig.5 (*top right*). The waste strips are then removed.

Fig.6 (*second from top*). The wall under the join is pasted.

Fig.7 (*third from top*). The edges of the fabric are pressed into position.

Fig.8 (*bottom*). The excess fabric at the top and bottom of the wall is trimmed off.

Above. Gingham fabric makes a gay wallcovering in the kitchen in places not likely to be splashed.
Below. On a plain door, brass tacks are

a decorative finish to fabric panels.
Opposite, above. Panelled doors are ideal for picking out in fabric. You can achieve a similar effect with a cut-out frame.

PAUL REDMAN

(Fig.10). Always cut first through the top surface of a moulding. Cut the other piece in the same way and to the same length. Smooth all edges.

If you have no mitre board or bench hook, you could even improvize a bench hook quite easily. Then mark the beading to the exact length of the frame, leaving about 1in. of 'waste' on each end for easy handling. Measure the width of the beading exactly, and measure the same distance in from the ends along the outer edge. At this point, mark another line—with pencil—across the beading parallel to the first line. Check that the distance between the lines is exactly the same as the width of the beading, and then mark the beginning and end of a diagonal line—this will be the cutting line (Fig.10). Hold the beading on the bench hook and then cut off the ends as above.

Lightly tack the lengths in position with three panel pins—two about 1in. from each end and one in the middle—but without driving them completely home (the gap between the beading and surface should be the thickness of the beading). Cut two more pieces of beading to match the width of the frame, plus 2in. Gently wedge these pieces in position behind the upright pieces of beading (Fig.11). Check that the frame is square by measuring the diagonals (they should be equal).

Use a handyman's knife or other sharp knife to scribe the angled cutting lines on the top and bottom pieces so that they join the side pieces exactly. Then remove all the beading, being careful not to tear the side pieces. Cut the top and bottom pieces, smooth the edges, and then paint or varnish all the pieces. When completely dry, check that the pieces still fit together perfectly and make any necessary adjustments.

Cut the fabric to the inside size of the frame, plus $\frac{1}{8}$in. To make sure edges are square, pull a thread for each side and then cut along it. Pull a piece at the opposite corner if it still is not square. Starch the fabric to give it body and then secure it smoothly in position using staples or double-sided adhesive tape. If there is a possibility of the fabric stretching, leave it for a few days and cut and re-position if necessary. Then tack down the beading to cover the fabric $\frac{1}{8}$in. all round with panel pins at 3in.-4in. intervals, and touch up the paint where necessary.
Braid edging

Mark the area of the frame and cut a length of braid to fit the perimeter, plus $\frac{3}{4}$in. Mark the position of the corners and mitre the corners very carefully, cutting off any excess braid. Cut out the fabric and secure it in position as above and then, using a latex-based adhesive, stick down the braid to cover the fabric edges. Join the braid by turning under the edges and making a butt join.

Opposite (Fig.9). With a plywood frame the fabric is tacked down and its edges are covered by the inner edge of the frame.
Fig.10. If you have no mitre board, a 45° angle can be made by first marking a line parallel to, and at a distance of the beading's width, from the end. The diagonal is the cutting line.
Fig.11. To make a perfect join, mark the cutting line for the top and bottom of the frame when the side struts are in position.

MICHAEL BOYS

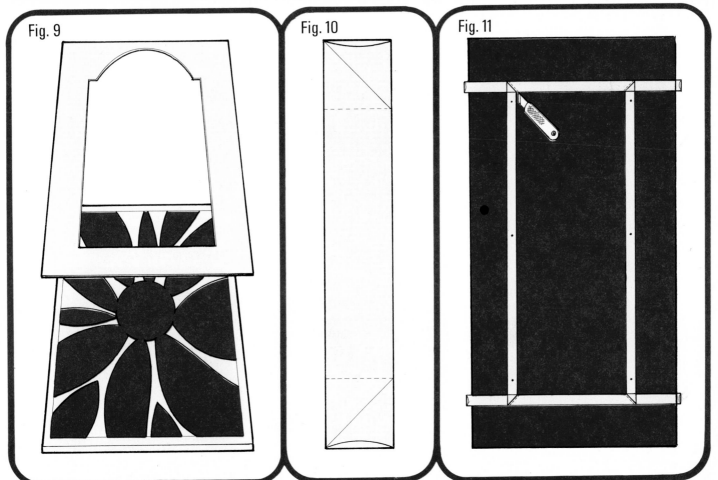

Fig. 9

Fig. 10

Fig. 11

Linoleum and vinyl flooring

Today, it is an easy task to lay sheet flooring, and an even easier one to maintain it. Whether you choose linoleum or a newer, vinyl flooring, the techniques are virtually the same—and will take a few hours only. Furthermore, sheet flooring comes in a range of designs, suitable for almost any decor.

Linoleum

When linoleum was first produced more than 100 years ago, it tended to be coarse and rather unsightly, but changes in manufacturing techniques have resulted in a flooring material which is, today, as attractive looking as vinyl.

Linoleum is made from oxidized linseed oil, cork dust and/or wood flour, pigments, gums and resins which are mixed together and rolled under pressure on to a hessian or felt backing. The rolled sheet is then left to cure and toughen.

Linoleum flooring is flexible, smooth surfaced, resilient and extremely durable. It is warm to the touch, absorbs impact sounds to a degree, and resists general hard wear and ordinary household staining, including fats and oils. Alcohol, however, can affect the surface if left on it for too long.

Many patterns and colours are available in sheet and tile linoleum, ranging from plain colours, marbleized effects and printed and inlaid patterns, to wood-grain-like planks or parquet-type inlays. Normally produced in 6ft. (1.83m) widths, linoleum comes in various grades from a 2.50mm (.10in.) thickness, suitable for light traffic areas, to 3.2mm (.12in.) thickness, suitable for hard wear. Even thicker grades are produced, mainly for contract use, to resist extremely heavy traffic.

Although linoleum is slightly thicker than unbacked vinyl flooring and is generally very resilient, it should still be laid on a very flat sub-floor, or joints and small bumps and imperfections in the floor will eventually show through and even crack the surface. Hardboard at least $\frac{1}{8}$in. (3mm) thick or resin-bonded plywood, which is slightly more expensive, should be used to cover the floor, unless it has already been sanded smooth. In this case, it is sometimes sufficient to cover it with two layers of a felt paper.

Linoleum is best fixed with the recommended adhesive; if you loose-lay or tack it, water may seep under the joins and rot the hessian or jute backing. If loose laying cannot be avoided, attach a strip of 2in. (50mm) wide self-adhesive cotton tape to the underside of the joins for added protection.

Linoleum has a tendency to stretch slightly once it has been laid, so permanent fixing should not be completed until the sheet has been down for at least seven to ten days.

Vinyl sheet—unbacked

Rivalling linoleum, unbacked vinyl is one of the most popular smooth sheet floorcoverings. It is durable, flexible, hard-wearing and fairly resilient, although it does not absorb sounds to the same degree as linoleum, and it is cold to the touch. If it is laid on a smooth, dry and firm floor, it will give years of service, and it has much to recommend it on the practical side, as it shrugs off dirt, grease and alkali stains, and is unaffected by surface moisture. Unbacked vinyl retains its colour, patterned effects and surface sheen virtually to the end of its life.

Bathrooms, kitchens and nurseries are ideal places to use a vinyl sheet flooring because it is so easy to clean. Apart from floors, sheet vinyl can also be used as a surface for desk and dressing table tops, or it may even be fixed to walls. However, it is suitable for kitchen worktops only if you are careful not to allow hot pans to damage the surface.

Sheet vinyl comes in various grades, ranging from pure vinyl (pvc) to vinyl that has been mixed with various fillers and other constituents. These are available in thicknesses from 1.6mm to 2.5mm (.06in. to .10in.) and in widths from 3ft to 12ft (.91m to 3.66m), and the extra large width of 12ft (3.66m).

Unlike linoleum, which stretches a little after being put down, vinyl has a tendency to shrink across the *width* of the sheet. To compensate for this, the flooring should be cut slightly over-size and allowed to settle for at least a week before being trimmed to fit the room contours.

Backed vinyl

Sheet vinyl also comes with a cushioned backing, giving the flooring both the practicability of a hardwearing surface and a spongy comfort underfoot. It is warmer to the touch and quieter to walk on than either linoleum or unbacked vinyl. Normally, the surfaces are slightly textured, which provides a good grip, especially when the floor is wet. Cushioned vinyl flooring is as easy to maintain and just as durable as its 'plain' alternative—a damp mop over will remove surface grime without spoiling the sheen.

Sheet vinyls are cushioned with a number of different materials—latex/asbestos, foamed vinyl layers, even compressed felt. The more layers that are used, the more expensive the actual finished flooring will be. This cushioning helps to shrug off heavy impressions and indentations fairly quickly, but it is still advisable to use castor cups under heavy furniture to avoid permanent flattening of the surface. Also, avoid

dropping cigarettes or lighted matches on to the surface, or to set any hot instruments, such as irons, on to a vinyl surface, as it will melt.

The designs for backed vinyl flooring make it generally more attractive to use in living rooms or bedrooms than other types of sheet flooring. It is less hard looking and has a lightly im-

printed surface. It is not usually used as a substitute for carpeting, but it does make an attractive and comfortable flooring to combine with carpets. Cushioned vinyls can be laid on all floors except those which are prone to rising damp. However, as mentioned above, it is always best to put down a sub-floor to protect

any type of floor covering which is used.

Like sheet vinyls, cushioned vinyls · are available in a variety of thicknesses and usually in widths of 6ft and 12ft (1.83m and 3.66m). When laying cushioned vinyls, you will need to secure the joins with an adhesive to prevent water from seeping into the backing. If

Above. *Modern vinyl materials have made it possible to cover nearly any type of floor with a colourful, comfortable and durable surface. The traditional-looking, timber panelled room, seen above, is given the final, appropriate touch with a modern, soft blue, patterned sheet flooring.*

47

Fig.1. *It is usually easiest to begin near a doorway. Butt the first piece up close to the skirting and measure the distance from midway in the doorway.*

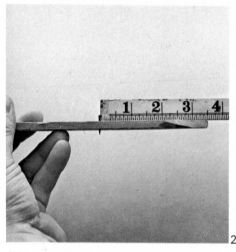

Fig.2. *Next measure off the same distance, in this case 3½in. (88.9mm), on to a pointed piece of wood and drive a nail through the wood, or scribing tool, to mark the place.*

Fig.3. *Pull the scriber along the sheet of flooring, holding it firmly against the skirting. This action traces off the same distance measured from midway in the doorway.*

Fig.5. *Continue tracing out the shape of the architrave, moving into the curves and marking off the measurement on to the strip of flooring with the scriber.*

Fig.6. *After marking out all the distances, take a straight rule and a felt-tipped pen and fill in all the marks at right angles to your original line.*

Fig.7. *The traced outline of the architrave moulding transferred out on to the strip of flooring, with all the measurements kept in exact proportions.*

Fig.9. *Move the sheet in against the skirting and around the architrave. If you have measured properly, it will be a perfect fit. Leave an overlap at the far wall.*

Fig.10. *Once the flooring has settled, you may scribe any overlaps to fit. First make a mark down the skirting board and continue it along the flooring so it is clearly seen.*

Fig.11. *Now move the flooring back so that the overlapped end just touches the skirting board. Measure the distance that you have moved it—ie, between the two marked lines.*

Fig.4. When you come to the edge of the architrave, you must trace off its exact shape to the correct measurements. Hold the scriber against the moulding and make a mark.

Fig.8. Now, using a handyman's knife, cut out the architrave shape on the flooring. Then continue cutting along the straight line scribed parallel to the skirting.

Fig.12. Position the pin in the scriber to correspond with this distance and holding it against the skirting, trace out a line to this distance at the overlapped edge.

professionally laid, this flooring can be cold or hot welded to make a completely seamless floor.

Conditioning

All sheet floorings should be kept indoors for at least two days, preferably longer, before being laid. This conditions them to the indoor temperature and moisture content, and makes them more flexible and easier to handle when being laid. This is particularly so with linoleum, which can crack if it is too cold.

Laying sub-floors

Before laying of sheet flooring, you should inspect and correct any faults in the floor. Generally speaking, if you have a solid concrete floor make sure it is dry and level; all dents and cracks must be filled in and high spots sanded smooth. If there are any signs of damp, the cause must be traced and eliminated.

When covering suspended timber flooring, check to see that all joints and boards are clear of damp rot or fungus. High spots and nail heads should be attended to, and loose boards nailed down tight.

If you are laying a sub-floor on to the original floor surface, make sure that the floorboards underneath are well ventilated; air bricks and grilles in your exterior walls should be completely clear. Flooring grade hardboard or ordinary $\frac{1}{8}$ in. (3mm) thick hardboard which has been correctly tempered are both quite suitable for use as sub-floor coverings because they are durable and firm enough to take the weight and expanse of sheet flooring.

Before you actually lay the sub-floor, make certain that the doors into the room will still be able to open. If not, they will have to be taken off their hinges so that their bases can be planed down. If you forget to check this detail and put down the new sub-floor first, it may be impossible to remove the doors to adjust them to the new level.

Calculating quantities

Since most sheet materials are available in 6ft (1.83m) widths, it is fairly simple to work out how much material you will need for a room. For example, the calculations for a room 12ft wide x 10ft long (3.66m x 3.05m) to be fitted with material 6ft (1.83m) wide are: 12ft divided by 6ft equals 2ft. Multiply 2ft by the length of the room (10ft), and the result is 20ft (6.09m) of sheet flooring necessary.

To take another example, if the room were only 9ft (2.74m) wide by 13ft (3.96m) long, one width of flooring might be cut down the middle to keep wastage to a minimum. This would be calculated as follows: 9ft divided by 6ft equals 1½ft. Multiply by the length of the room: 1½ft x 13ft equals 19½ft of flooring needed. Be certain, however, to purchase enough flooring to allow for a 2in. (50mm) overlap to match patterns and at least 2in. extra around edges to allow for cutting in.

Before choosing the sheet flooring, decide which way the floorcovering is to run, so that joins are avoided in doorways where they are clearly seen and might be kicked up.

Tools and materials

The basic tools for laying sheet flooring are a hammer, handyman's knife and straightedge.

For laying *vinyl, backed or unbacked,* you will need **1**, A piece of wood about 6in. wide to use as a guide block. **2**, Latex-based adhesive for seaming, or double-sided adhesive tape. **3**, Vinyl adhesive and spreader if all-over fixing is to be carried out.

For laying *linoleum,* you will need: **1**, A special curved lino knife. **2**, A hammer and gimp pins, or special lino brads, for tacking. **3**, Linoleum adhesive for all-over fixing. **4**, Carpet tape for strengthening joint edges when loose laying.

Laying sheet flooring

The techniques for laying all sheet flooring materials is virtually the same. For vinyls, both backed and unbacked, joins should be lapped by about ½in. (12.7mm) with at least a surplus of 1½in. (38.1mm) extra left around the edges, to allow for shrinkage. Linoleum should be cut to fit to exact sizes, since it will spread rather than shrink.

Vinyls

Begin by cutting the first width of vinyl 2in. (50.8mm) longer than the length needed. Lay this strip parallel to the longest wall, but about 5in. (127mm) away from it, and allow the ends of this piece to ride up 1in. (25.4mm) on each end wall.

Next, take your 6in. (152mm) wide block of wood. Place it in a corner against the longest wall, so that one edge butts against the skirting board and the other overlaps on to the vinyl by about 1in. (25.4mm). Hold a pencil against the outside edge of the block, and begin moving the block and pencil along from the corner, so that a mark is made on the vinyl which follows the contours of the skirting exactly. Cut along this line with a handyman's knife (and straight edge where you strike straight sections), remove the surplus material and fit the length flush against the skirting.

You can now lay subsequent lengths of flooring alongside the first. Make a minimum overlap of ½in. (12.7mm) along the sides of adjoining pieces—more, if you need more to make the pattern match. These overlaps will be cut through and butted together at a later stage. Always be *certain* that your pattern matches along lengths.

When you reach the wall on the opposite side of the room from your original wall, you will need to scribe the sheet to fit evenly along the wall. There are two ways to tackle this:

1, Lay your vinyl a few inches from the wall, use a scribing block and pencil to mark your cutting line, and score along the line with a handyman's knife. (Allow a 'whisker' extra to allow for the thickness of the pencil mark).

2, Lay your vinyl a foot or two from the wall—this is sometimes necessary when you must work around a built-in fitment; measure the distance from the wall at several points; join these points with a pencil mark to make your cutting line; and cut as before.

With either method you use, the important points to remember are:

1, You must lay your vinyl so that the pattern on the sheet you are marking matches *exactly* the pattern on the sheet underneath; otherwise,

Fig.13. *Hold the straight edge firmly against this line and cut it with a handyman's knife. (You are actually cutting off the excess measured between the two lines).*

Fig.14. *On all sheet flooring, it is necessary to trim seams to make butt joins. Be sure the pattern matches, overlap the two pieces by 1in. and cut through the middle.*

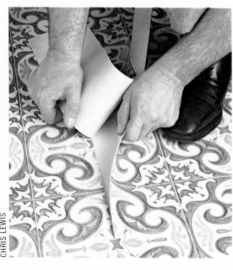

CHRIS LEWIS

Fig.15. *When you have cut through the middle of both overlapped pieces, lift them up and carefully pull the excess away. The remaining seam should be a smooth butt.*

your pattern will be 'out' after you have cut it.

2, The width of your scribing block must be *exactly* the same as the amount of overlap between the sheet you are cutting and the sheet below it. For example, if you have moved your vinyl in 4½in. from where it will finally be laid, you must use a block 4½in. wide. (In effect, you are 'moving' both vinyl and wall 4½in. from where they will finally be.) Forget about the amount you must cut off; what counts is the amount you *have left*. Similarly, if you have had to lay your vinyl 1ft 8⅜in. from where it will finally go, you should have an overlap of 1ft 8⅜in., and all the marks you measure from the wall or cupboard should be 1ft 8⅜in.

Fitting awkward areas

To fit pieces of flooring around awkward shapes, protuberances or door architraves, it is first necessary to make a paper template of the shape to be cut out. Use a piece of heavy brown paper or cardboard to make the template and butt it up against the shape to be cut around. Tape it to the floor and trace off the exact shape using the correct measurements.

The actual process of making a template is extremely important for the correct fitting of your flooring and it is mainly one of trial and error, so be sure to take the time and care necessary to do it accurately.

Proprietary metal templates are available which look like combs with adjustable teeth. These allow you to press the teeth against the shape to be copied, reproducing the exact outline on the outside edge. This outline can then be transferred to the material and the shape traced out and cut out. These may be useful to use around awkward shaped door architraves.

Cutting

Allow the flooring to settle before trimming it to fit exactly. The more time you can allow, the better—between four and six days is sufficient if the room is frequently used, between eight and ten days if it is seldom used.

Joins

Once the vinyl has settled, check to see that the two scribed edges are flush with the skirting. If not, adjust them by moving the outside sheets. Now, using a straightedge, cut through both sheets at the middle point of the overlapped section at each joint, using a handyman's knife (see Fig.14). Remove the surplus strips and ease the two edges down; they should butt together perfectly.

Edges

Once the joins have been trimmed to fit, you may trim the ends of the vinyl to fit along the skirting. Again, this should be done by the principle of scribing. Figs.9 to 13 give step-by-step details of how this should be done.

Bonding

Full instructions for bonding are usually supplied with the floorcoverings. However, the following will act as a guide. All bonding is done once the vinyl has settled and has been trimmed to fit.

All-over bonding is sometimes recommended for cushioned vinyls. To do this, spread about a

yard (.91m) of adhesive at a time. Begin in a corner, spread it evenly and lay the first strip. Bond the joins carefully at the next strip (spread more adhesive if necessary) by kneeling on the finished part and pulling the second, loose strip towards you. Use a heavy weight, such as an unheated electric iron or heavy book, to smooth the vinyl into place, and to expel all air beneath the flooring. Continue working in this way, checking as you go to see that all joins are even.

For loose-laying, use double-sided adhesive tape under each trimmed join to prevent the edges from curling back or from being kicked up. Alternatively, you may run a 3in. (76.2mm) wide seam of latex adhesive under the join and press the edges of the flooring to it. A wallpaper seam roller will help to smooth the joins.

Once the seams have been bonded, the outer edges which are at right angles to the seams should be fixed. Bond one side with the latex adhesive and allow it to set for a couple of days. Then bond the opposite side in the same way. Do not bond the edges which are parallel to the seams as these must be left loose to allow for any possible movement.

Linoleum fitting

The techniques described for laying vinyl apply to lino fitting as well, except that linoleum should be cut to fit initially. It will spread, rather than shrink, once it has been put down. Allow it to settle and spread for at least a week, preferably longer, then trim it off to fit.

If left loose laid, double-sided adhesive tape on the floor will hold the joins firmly. An added protection along the outer edges is to use carpet tape. In the case of linoleum all edges should be fixed with tape, not just those parallel to the seams.

If tacking is preferred, special lino nails or gimp pins should be fixed at 6in. (152mm) intervals, pinned about ¼in. (6.35mm) in from the skirting board all round the floor.

The best permanent method for fixing is to use an all-over bond with the special adhesive recommended by the linoleum manufacturer.

Maintenance

A floorcovering will give good service if it is properly cleaned and protected. Today, this involves little effort or time.

Linoleum will take any good wax polish, although special polishes are sometimes recommended by the manufacturers which contain certain oils and other constituents to feed the surface and keep it supple. Dry mop frequently to remove dust. When washing, use mild soaps and detergents; harsh solutions and abrasives will only scratch and dry out the surface, making it brittle and prone to cracking. Remember, do not over-wet the surface.

Vinyls, both plain and cushioned, simply need an occasional damp mop over the surface with a mild detergent or soap solution to keep them looking bright. Occasionally, a water-based wax emulsion can be used to provide added 'sparkle', but it is not a necessary practice. Never use harsh abrasives, paraffin or turpentine as they will damage the vinyl surface.

Properly cared for, your floorcovering will repay your initial expense with years of wear.

Plastic laminates have revolutionized modern decorative finishes. They are easy to clean, stain resistant, and simple to apply. For worktops and splashbacks few other materials can compare.

Plastic laminates are extremely versatile as a decorative medium. A kaleidoscope of designs, patterns and colours is available—wood grains, linen and cloth effects, marble, agate and mosaic patterns, and hundreds of other designs from stripes to gingham checks.

Handling plastic laminates

Laminates are made up from several sheets of paper, ranging from the heavy brown kraft paper of the core to the decorative surface paper, all impregnated with resins under extreme heat and pressure. This makes a single sheet of a hard dense material.

The hardwearing, resilient nature of laminates, resistant to both heat and stains, makes them an ideal finish for working surfaces about the house. However, strong chemicals, such as household bleach, peroxide and some solvents should be avoided at all costs, as these can badly damage the surface. Strong abrasive cleaners, caustic soda and even some fruit juices can also be harmful and should be wiped clean immediately.

Buying and storing

Laminates available for do-it-yourself work commonly come in two thicknesses. Sheets $\frac{1}{16}$in. (1.5mm) thick are for surfaces which must take hard wear, while sheets $\frac{1}{32}$in. (1mm) thick are for less 'busy' places, such as linings.

Standard sheet sizes are 8ft x 4ft (2.44m x 1.22m), 9ft x 4ft (2.74m x 1.22m), 10ft x 4ft (3.05m x 1.22m), and an extra large size of 13ft 6in. x 5ft (4.12m x 1.52m) is available.

The most economical way to buy (apart from off-cuts for small jobs) is to buy large sheets, from which you cut pieces for several jobs. Buying cut-to-size laminates can cost 50 per cent more.

Before buying your large sheets of laminate, check whether edging strips are available in the same colour; these can save a lot of time.

If you do not wish to use ready-made edging strips, or cannot buy them, there are several alternatives: plastic strips, metal strips, and wooden mouldings in a variety of profiles.

Keep laminate sheets inside the house for a day or two before using them, to acclimatize them to the temperature. Keep them away from newly-plastered (and therefore, probably damp) walls. Always store the sheets flat—stood on end, they will bow out of shape and possibly become chipped along the edges.

Preparing the surfaces

Materials such as chipboard, blockboard and plywood, which offer a continuous surface—without joints to open and close as humidity varies—are ideal for laminating.

To provide a good key for the adhesive, surfaces should be smooth, dry and grease-free. Painted or varnished surfaces must be stripped or sanded down to bare wood.

Unless the boards you are laminating are going to be screwed to a framework which will hold them rigid they should be laminated on both sides. The backing laminate, if it will not be visible in the finished job, can be a cheap, thin variety. It will provide stability and help counter the 'pull' of the facing laminate, which might otherwise warp the board.

Measuring and marking out

For economy's sake, always plan the layout of cuts on your laminate sheet carefully, in much the same way as a dressmaker or tailor does with a length of cloth. Wrong pencil lines can be wiped clean and re-marked; wrong cuts cannot!

Unless you propose to cut with a jig-saw (see below), mark out by laying the laminate sheet on a flat, level and dry surface, with the decorative face upwards. The floor will serve, or a large table, provided its surface is well protected with old hardboard or a similar hard sheeting to prevent accidental scratches and cuts.

For *rectangular* shapes, use a pencil and steel straight-edge, or any piece of straight timber at least $\frac{1}{4}$in. (6mm) thick, to mark cutting lines. Measure at least $\frac{1}{8}$in. (3mm) all round over the size required, so that you have a margin for trimming later.

For *round* or *irregular* shapes, you will need to run your pencil around the outside of a template. The best template is the actual piece of board to which the laminate is to be stuck. Remember to place it right way up on the laminate when you are marking the face laminate, but upside down when you are marking the backing laminate.

If at all possible, cut out any awkward shapes while the boards are available as templates (for cutting methods, see below).

If you cannot 'direct mark' in this way, you will have to make a template from sheet metal or (at a pinch) cardboard, and mark around that.

Cutting tools

Laminates can be cut with several different kinds of tools. Whichever you choose, always cut through the face side first to avoid flaking away the decorative surface.

A sharp, fine-toothed *veneer saw* or *tenon saw* is fine for small jobs, although on large jobs the saw will quickly become blunt.

A *handyman's knife* with a laminate-cutting blade can be used to deep-score along the line to be cut. So can a tungsten-tipped *straight laminate cutter*, whose extra hard, sharp edge bites deeply into the laminate surface and makes long, straight cutting easy.

Power tools can also be used, provided that they are not forced through the laminate but allowed to cut their way easily. *Carborundum-edged discs* can be bought to fit both bench saws and portable saws. A *jig-saw* can also be used, but because it cuts on the *up* stroke the laminate should be laid face down while you cut it. Do not work too closely if you use power tools, since tiny splinters of laminate can fly upwards and injure an eye.

Cutting: scoring method

Remember always to allow $\frac{1}{8}$in. (3mm) extra all round for later trimming.

If you are cutting a large sheet, you can use a short straight-edge for a series of overlapping strokes, but a long one is better.

Lay the straight-edge in place along the pencil line and keep it steady with one hand. Using a handyman's knife or straight laminate cutter, start scoring gently from one end of the sheet. Hold the cutting blade or tool against the edge of the straight-edge to keep it straight while it travels along the entire length of the pencilled guide line. Do this at least three or four times, increasing the pressure of cut each time, until the dark under-surface of the laminate appears as a clean, unbroken line.

Work steadily, and do not rush. If you apply too much pressure at the first few strokes, you might cut into the straight-edge, or your cutting tool could slip, damaging the surface away from the cutting line.

Once the dark score line shows, remove the straight-edge and continue scoring in the deepening line—the knife will not slip out now —until the whole line is cut through.

Alternatively, after fairly deep scoring, keep the straight-edge in place, holding it firm with one hand. With the other hand, snap the laminate piece clean by lifting the free edge and bending it upwards. This 'snap' method, unless you are experienced, is good only for short lengths. Long offcuts will sometimes snap in half unless they are adequately supported.

Cutting: sawing method

Remember always allow $\frac{1}{8}$in. (3mm) extra all round for later trimming.

Put the laminate sheet on a flat, sturdy trestle, workbench or table, with its decorative face upwards and the pencilled guide lines slightly overhanging the edge.

If the strip to be cut off is more than 3in. (76mm) wide, this too must be supported or the laminate will break away. Use another table or trestle.

Begin by scoring along the pencilled line with a scriber or handyman's knife as a guide for the saw cut. When you start sawing, hold the saw at a 'flat' angle—20°, no more. If you try to cut at a sharper angle the sheet will vibrate and 'chatter' as the saw teeth catch and pull. Saw gently and slowly along the marked line, holding the main laminate sheet steady with your other hand. Do not try to go too fast, since rough treatment can cause flaking of the decorative surface.

When you have only 3in. (76mm) or so left to cut, you must take extra care to see that the corner edge does nor tear away. Saw across the surface until the dark under-surface shows as an unbroken line. Then hold the off-cut while you ease the saw blade through the last few strokes.

Curved, as well as straight, lines can be cut in this way—although, for very tight curves, you will have to use a series of short, straight cuts and finish off later with a file.

Cutting awkward shapes

Cutting irregular shapes, circles and curves from laminate is not difficult. It can be tackled in two ways.

Before you begin, your template has to be absolutely accurate—and the usual $\frac{1}{8}$in. over-size—as the laminate cannot easily be trimmed back to fit without risking damage to the material.

The first method is to put the template in position on the laminate and hold it in place with strips of folded cellulose adhesive tape placed between the face of the laminate and the back of the template. Trace round the outline with a metal scriber (or handyman's knife held vertically), increasing the pressure steadily each full circuit, until a clean, unbroken, dark score line appears.

Remove the template, insert into the (now fairly deep) groove either the handyman's knife or the straight laminate cutter, and continue scoring until you have cut right through the surface, and the shape comes away cleanly with no fractured edges.

The second method is to drill carefully,

around the outline, a series of fine holes. These perforations can then be pierced with a fine-toothed keyhole saw, or power jig-saw, and the traced outline sawn to shape. The edges will have to be smoothed down and polished with wire wool and some light household oil.

Adhesives for laminates

Three types of adhesives will bond laminates well: impact (or contact) adhesive; synthetic resins; and epoxy-based adhesives.

Impact adhesives are allowed to become touch dry before the surfaces to be joined together are 'mated'. Once the surfaces are pressed together, they stick fast. This is an advantage, in that you do not needs cramps or weights to hold the surfaces together while the adhesive dries. It is also a disadvantage, in that you have no margin for error—if the laminate goes down crooked, it will *stay* crooked. There is another disadvantage: although in cold weather it may take 30 minutes for the adhesive to 'go off'—that is, dry out sufficiently for you to

---

Where you can use laminates

In the kitchen: work surfaces; table tops; shelves; insides and outsides of cupboards; drawer fronts and interiors; splashbacks behind sink and cooker; toe boards of cupboards; trays and cutting boards; and—to eliminate painting—skirting boards, window sills, and the wall areas between worktops and eye-level cupboards.

In the bathroom or laundry: bath panels; wall and ceiling linings; sink and bath splashbacks; shower cubicle linings; vanitory unit surfaces; skirting boards and window sills.

In other rooms: shelf surfaces; table tops; strip-lighting baffles; cupboards and wardrobe doors; desk tops; dressing-table tops.

---

attempt a bond—in hot weather it can take only 4 or 5 minutes, which means you must work very quickly indeed.

Synthetic resin adhesives, unlike impact adhesives, allow plenty of time for positioning, and the laminate can be adjusted and readjusted, if necessary. Their disadvantage is that even pressure must be applied throughout the drying time to achieve a firm bond between the laminate and the under-surface. This can take hours, depending on the room's temperature. However, the overall bond is very good and tends to be more water- and heat-resistant than that obtained from impact adhesives.

Epoxy-based adhesives are 'two-pot' adhesives, made from a base and a hardener which you mix together. Like synthetic resin adhesives, they require even pressure throughout their drying-out time. The resulting bond is completely waterproof.

Glueing laminates

The most important thing about applying adhesive to laminates is to spread an absolutely even coat over the whole surface; otherwise, air pockets may form and cause the laminate to 'bubble' slightly.

Particularly if you are working with impact adhesive, or over a large area, the plastic spreader supplied by the adhesive manufacturer may be hopelessly inadequate for this job. So the first step is to make yourself a bigger spreader, with a serrated edge like the one supplied. You can use any stiff material for this—for example, an off-cut of the laminate itself, notched with a saw.

The next step is to check below to make sure that you have all the equipment needed to position the laminate accurately and, if necessary, to weight it down and/or clamp it. Equip yourself also with some solvent (the back of the adhesive tin will tell you which) so that any spilled adhesive can be wiped off the surface of the laminate immediately.

Then, before applying the adhesive to the laminate and the surface which will receive it, you should do a 'test-run' on aligning and positioning accurately the pieces of laminate. You can do this in two ways. One is to push drawing pins into the timber, on both sides of one corner angle, to act as guide stops. The laminate is then rested on the surface against the pins and the sheet is aligned. Any adjustment of the slight overhang for trimming can be done by easing out the pins until the laminate projects evenly all round the board.

The other method is to place pieces of wood lath over the surface to be covered (they should be at least the width of the board you are covering) and position the cut laminate over the laths.

Using impact adhesive

Pour the adhesive down the middle of the laminate sheet—on the back, of course—and spread it thinly with the spreader. Draw it out to each side, making sure that the sides and edges are amply covered. Work quickly, as the adhesive can start to thicken up in minutes. Be sure to work in a well-ventilated area and avoid excessive heat, as this adhesive is highly inflammable.

Repeat the process on the board surface to be covered. Leave both surfaces until the adhesive is touch dry; any patches of wet adhesive trapped below the laminate will cause a breakdown in the bond.

If you are using the drawing pin positioning method, put a piece of greaseproof paper between the laminate sheet and the board surface, and ease the end of the laminate into position against the drawing pins in the corner. Now withdraw the paper with one hand as you 'roll' the laminate down on to the surface with the other, pressing the laminate down hard as you go along. By rolling, you prevent any air from getting underneath and interfering with the bond.

If you are using the wooden lath positioning method, lay the laths on the board you are covering—they will not stick—and lay the laminate sheet on top of the laths. Stick down about 2in. of laminate at one edge, and slip out the laths, one by one, to allow the laminate to be rolled down, firmly pressing as you go.

Using synthetic resin glue

Mix the adhesive following the maker's instructions, and spread it in the same way as for impact adhesive. Use only enough adhesive so that it just oozes out along the edges when pressure is applied. Slide the laminate panels into position and adjust them as necessary.

With this type of adhesive, you need to apply all-over pressure along the whole surface during the curing time, which depends on the room temperature. Put a sheet of hardboard or chipboard over the decorative surface to protect its face from damage, and to help spread an even pressure over the whole area. For large areas, apply the pressure by stacking heavy books, bricks, paving slabs—or even heavy furniture—on the hardboard cover.

Only when the glue beads exuded around the edges have set do you release the pressure. The glue beads can be trimmed off with a sharp knife.

Using epoxy resin adhesive

It is important with epoxy resins that the surfaces to be covered must be absolutely grease-free, or the adhesive will not work.

Mix the adhesive according to the manufacturer's instructions; then proceed as you would with a synthetic resin.

Trimming

Once the adhesive has dried, the $\frac{1}{8}$in. of overhang on the edges of the laminate has to be trimmed flush. To do this, use a small, sharp block plane, the blade set at a fine trim. A wrongly set or blunt blade will produce a 'chewed' or 'torn' edge, and possibly chipping. Work 'from ends to middle'. Plane slowly, using smooth, sweeping strokes until the edge is flush with the board below. For a really smooth finish, rub down after trimming with wire wool and a fine-grade oil.

Another method of trimming is to use a fine, flat file, held at a slight diagonal angle. Work downwards, from the face edge of the laminate. If you stroke upwards you will pull away the decorative face and may cause chipping. A third method is to use a medium-grade glasspaper, wrapped tightly around a wood block. Use the same technique as for filing.

Edging

Professionals fix on edgings before the main surfaces, because less of the brown core shows and there is less chance of the edge veneer accidentally being pulled away. Some handymen find it easier to work the other way round, doing the more difficult large areas first.

Cut the laminate edging slightly oversize in width and length and use the adhesive in the same way as you did for the main sheet. With impact adhesive, no great pressure is needed after the surfaces are touch dry; they will 'mate' immediately. Where the other adhesives are used, edging cramps will hold the trims in place. Use a batten of 2in. x 1in. (50mm x 25mm) timber between the cramps and the laminate, and space the cramps at 6in. (152mm) intervals.

Alternatively, for short edging strips you may use pieces of sticky tape to hold the laminate in place until the glue bonds.

If you are using a timber edging, sand it smooth before fixing it. This prevents the glasspaper from scratching the laminate.

A brighter front door

The front door is the part of a house that people see first when they visit. If your front door is blistered and peeling, with dirty glass or stained stonework, be sure that observant and critical eyes will be taking note of the front. But it is really very easy to make the shabbiest doorway look smart again.

Front doors suffer from a variety of faults, the commonest of which is that the paintwork is in bad condition. Other troubles include the door not opening and closing properly, dirty frosted-glass panes, tatty wooden thresholds and, if there is any stonework, iron stains and industrial grime. All these can easily be set right.

Varnished doors

Varnished doors, if they are to be revarnished- should not be stripped with a blowlamp as this chars the wood slightly. A good chemical paint stripper should be used for getting the varnish off. Always wear rubber gloves when using this corrosive chemical.

Most varnished doors will have a great deal of varnish on them, so don't expect the paint remover to work wonders. You may have to apply it several times to get all the varnish off. First remove all the door furniture (knockers etc.), then brush paint stripper all over the door, leave it to work for a quarter of an hour, then scrape the softened varnish off with a triangular shavehook for the flat panels and combination shavehook for the mouldings. Start at the top of the door and work down. Difficult mouldings may require coarse wire wool to get the last traces of varnish off.

Repeat this treatment as often as necessary until the wood is bare. Then wash the door carefully with warm water (no soap) to remove the stripper, or the new varnish will not bond to it.

Any gaps and cracks in the wood should then be filled. Don't use an ordinary cellulose filler (such as Polyfilla) for a wooden door because slamming the door will crack it. Use a special wood stopping (such as Brummer stopping) and tint it with emulsion paint tinters (these are brought in little tubes from paint shops) to match the wood. Holes over keyhole size, for example locks or letter plates which have been removed, can only be filled by cutting a matching wood block to shape and glueing it in with a waterproof urea formaldehyde glue (such as Aerolite), then planing if flush with the door surface. Make sure the grain on the patch runs the same way as the grain of the door.

When the surface of the door is repaired to your satisfaction, rub it down all over with fine glass paper and seal the grain with a half-and-half mixture of polyurethane varnish and turps substitute. Allow this to dry and rub it down again with fine paper, but not so hard as to wear through the thin coat.

Now apply a coat of neat varnish, not too thickly, or it will run. When it is dry, rub it down with 'flour grade' paper (the finest glass-paper). Repeat this at least twice until the surface is thickly coated and perfectly smooth, then apply a final coat of varnish without standing. The more coats you put on, the longer it will last.

Painted Doors

Stripping and repainting a painted door is less trouble, because the colour of the wood underneath does not have to be preserved. You can remove the paint quickly and easily with a blowlamp, taking all reasonable safety precautions, but be sure to remove all the door furniture before you begin or you will ruin it.

When the paint is all off, repair any damaged sections of the door. You can patch the smaller holes with ordinary plastic wood, because appearance does not matter provided the surface is smooth. Rub the whole door down with fine glasspaper, then apply wood primer, undercoat and several top coats.

Non-drip thixotropic gloss paint is very good for front doors, because ordinary paint tends to collect in drips along the lower edge of mouldings, no matter how carefully it is applied. It is worth while aiming for a really smooth gloss on a front door because it is a genuinely eye-catching feature.

Refitting the door

Old front doors are very prone to sticking in their frames. After all, they are exposed to the weather and are opened and shut more than any other door in the house, so it is not surprising that they tend to fail a bit sooner.

Sometimes it is the expansion of the door caused by damp air that makes it stick. The remedy for this is simple: plane a bit off the door where it is sticking. If the door jams badly, it is best to take the door off its hinges to do this; nothing looks worse than a badly-planned door edge. Fig.2 shows a useful aid for planing door edges. It is cut from a short length of 6in. x 2 ins. (150mm x 25mm) timber, and furnished with two wedges which grip the door.

Remember to repaint the exposed wood where you have planed, or moisture will rush in through the unprotected surface and make matters worse.

But don't assume, just because the door sticks, that it is too big for its frame. The trouble may just as well be caused by the hinges sagging, and if the door sticks along its lower edge, or along the top of the lock side, the chances are that this is the trouble. In this case, planing bits off the door will just make it draughtier.

Hinges generally sag because the screws are pulling out of their holes in the door frame. The simplest remedy, if the holes are only slightly worn, is to remove the door (with its hinges), put fibre plugs such as Rawplugs in the holes, and screw the hinges back. Place a dab of waterproof woodworking glue in the holes before you insert the fibre plugs, to ensure that they don't pull out. If the hinges are pulling out of the door as well, plug the holes there too.

If the frame is more extensively damaged,

there are two remedies. One is to take the hinges completely off and remount them nearer the middle of the door. Try to move them as little as possible; a top hinge that is set too low carries an abnormally high load and may come out again.

Moving the hinges in this way will involve you in cutting them into the door and frame, and re-hanging the door accurately, so don't attempt to do so unless you have to.

If the door frame is really badly split, the only thing you can do is let in a piece of new wood. This must have slanted ends, so that it holds itself in the frame while carrying the weight of the door (see fig. 1). Fasten it really firmly with waterproof glue and extra long screws which will hold it as securely as

Below. *Two stages in smartening up a doorway. The upper picture shows it before work started. In the lower one, the job is completed except for repairing the wall where the porch was, and painting the railings.*

possible. This is a long, skilled job, so don't do it unless there is no other way.

Brass Door Furniture

Most old doors have brass fittings that are black with age and look very shabby. But don't throw them away. Brass, unlike iron, does not rust and any brass fitting, however tarnished, can be made to sparkle again. The change is amazing. Even the most revolting old door furniture can be transformed into something to be proud of.

While all the fittings are off during the re-painting of the door, buy some oxalic acid from a chemist or colour merchant. It comes in crystal form. Make a strong solution with two tablespoonfuls to $\frac{1}{4}$ pint (100 ml) of water, and paint this on the surface of the brass. The acid is poisonous and corrosive; wear rubber gloves. After half an hour, wash it off with water and paint on more. Keep doing this until the brass is reasonably clean. It should only need two or three applications to remove all the old lacquer and dirt.

If the newly exposed surface of the brass is rough, smooth it with fine steel wool. Finish it off with brass polish, and re-lacquer it immediately (it begins to tarnish in minutes) with special brass lacquer or, failing that, any clear cellulose varnish. Do not touch unlacquered polished brass with your fingers, since the natural skin acids will make your fingerprints show up clearly in a few hours.

If some of your fittings are brass and some are steel, you could make the steel ones match the polished brass (more or less) by painting them with gold paint. Varnish over the top of the gilding (with clear polyuerthane varnish, not cellulose) to stop it from discolouring.

Cleaning glass

Cleaning dirt and paint smears off glass sounds easy, and if your door just has panels of plain glass in it, it is. A razor blade held nearly flat — watch your fingers! — peels off dirt and paint together. Many late Victorian and Edwardian houses, however, have stained glass panels in or beside the door.

Stained glass can be restored to its original brilliance with a nailbrush and weak solution of caustic soda. It is astonishing how colours that previously were not visible at all spring into life.

Take care, however, to protect the surrounding paintwork and floor covering from the corrosive solution, and wipe up any splashes immediately.

Old frosted glass of the usual design, where the surface is stamped with sharp-edged crystal patterns, is difficult to clean properly because dirt settles in the deep grooves. But paint stripper and a nailbrush will remove the paint, and a weak solution of caustic soda will clean the glass.

Wooden thresholds

Some houses have stone thresholds (see below) but most have a wooden one, generally made of oak or some other hardwood. This can get into a disreputable state, but whatever you do, don't paint it. The paint soon wears off and the last state is worse than the first.

The right way to clean a wooden threshold is to bleach it with the strongest possible solution of oxalic acid (see above under Brass door furniture) just go on putting crystals into the water until they won't dissolve any more, then paint this solution on the threshold. Leave

Below: Fig.1. A patch in a door frame to support a hinge must be set in really solidly, with slanted ends and long screws.
Fig.2. A simple door support to aid planing.

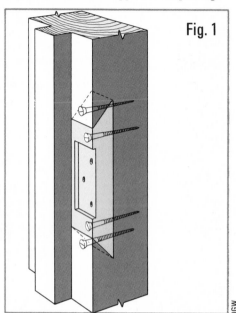

Fig. 1

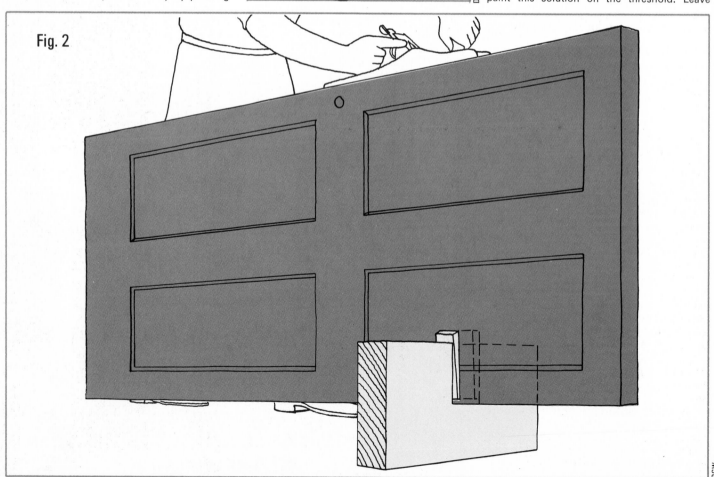

Fig. 2

Above. *The simple but colourful door of one of the cabins in the Munich Olympic village.*
Right. *Few houses boast an entrance as grand as this. But any panelled front door can be given added interest by painting the panels in a colour that contrasts with the frame.*

it a few hours, wash it off with plenty of water and re-apply as often as necessary.

Note the oxalic acid is extremely poisonous. A threshold may easily be licked by children or cats, so keep them away while you are cleaning it and wash it really thoroughly afterwards. Plain cold water washes as well as anything else.

When the threshold is dry, you might give it a few coats of colourless matt varnish and protect the edge with a screwed-on metal strip.

Stonework

Many doors in old masonry houses have stonework around the doors, as a frame or a threshold or both. In large towns, industrial grime makes this extremely dirty. Don't clean it with a wire brush; this ruins the surface.

The best way to clean stone is with a fairly weak solution of caustic soda and a nylon-bristled scrubbing brush. Wear rubber gloves. Some persistence may be required to get the stone clean, but it will come clean eventually and no other method is faster.

Iron stains—reddish marks where rainwater has brought down rust from iron fittings—can be removed quite quickly with a proprietary bath stain remover.

If you can't be bothered to scrub the stonework, or the stains are so ingrained that they just won't come out, the best thing to do is to paint the stone with a cement paint. This comes in a reasonably natural-looking stone colour in most brands.